Dawn at the summit of Mt. Kinabalu.

# General Introduction

Home to the largest known cave system in the world, the biggest flower, the largest undivided leaf, some of the world's rarest wildlife and the highest peak in South East Asia, along with vast tracks of rich and incredibly diverse rainforest fringed by some of the world's best coral reefs, the natural wonders of Borneo are truly superlative.

There are other superlatives too... the largest occupied palace and the biggest water village in the world, the first column-free building in Asia, some of the region's most renowned museums, centuries of tradition and culture and some of the most friendly and hospitable people you can hope to find, all combining to maintain Borneo's long-held reputation as one of the most alluring and exotic locations on earth.

Borneo is the world's third largest island after Greenland and New Guinea. Sarawak, Brunei Darussalam and Sabah together occupy about 28% of the total landmass of some 750,000 sq. km, with Indonesian Kalimantan forming the greater part of southern, central and eastern Borneo.

Sabah's magnificent rainforest.

Sarawak and Sabah comprise two of the thirteen states of the Federation of Malaysia. Known as 'East Malaysia', they are separated from Peninsular Malaysia by over 500 km of South China Sea at their nearest point. Sandwiched between Sarawak and Sabah is Brunei Darussalam, an Islamic Sultanate and one of South East Asia's oldest countries.

All three lie just above the equator, along the north western and northern flanks of Borneo. The climate is tropical - hot and humid throughout the year, with temperatures in the lowlands reaching 30°c - 32°c during the day. Temperatures decrease inside the rainforest, but the humidity increases noticeably. Two major monsoon winds influence rainfall patterns: the north east monsoon between October and February, and the generally less heavy south west monsoon from May to August. Typhoons miss the island of Borneo by several hundred kilometres, although the effect of their tailwinds may sometimes be experienced.

Regarded as relatively young geologically, the island of Borneo is thought to have emerged above sea level only about 15 million years ago, although some of the limestone rock formations found in eastern Sabah may be as much as 140 million years old.

About 2.5 million years ago, Borneo, Peninsular Malaysia, Sumatra and Java were all joined together, forming a continent known as Sundaland. Sea levels rose and fell, repeatedly exposing and submerging the land between the present day islands. The last ice age occurred about 15,000 years ago, when temperatures dropped a few degrees and vast quantities of water were locked up in the polar ice caps and mountain tops. This had the effect of decreasing the sea level as much as 150 metres below today's levels. At times like this, it would have been possible to walk from Borneo to Java and Sumatra and on up into Asia. Indeed these ancient land bridges facilitated migrations of both humans and animal and plant species, enriching the flora and fauna of the area. The present coastline of Borneo was formed sometime after the last ice age when sea levels rose again, thus isolating Borneo as an island once more.

# Journey through BORNEO

### Albert C.K. Teo

Text by:
## Sylvia Yorath

*Dedicated to my parents, my wife and
my children, whose sacrifices and encouragement
have made my journey through Borneo possible*

The Normah Orchid, *Phalaenopsis violacea*, Sarawak's state flower.

*Published by*
Sabah Handicraft Centre
Ground Floor, Lot 49, Bandaran Berjaya,
P. O. Box 12770, 88830 Kota Kinabalu, Sabah, Malaysia.
Tel: 60-88-232653

ISBN: 983-99612-6-8

*Typesetting and Design by*
Prestige Advertising Sdn Bhd
Kota Kinabalu

*Printed by*
Craft Print Pte Ltd
Singapore

# Message of the
## Honourable Minister of Culture,
## Arts and Tourism
## Malaysia

In the eyes of the foreign tourists, Malaysia has long been known for its beautiful sandy beaches, cultural diversity and exotic cuisines.

Due to the lack of information, many do not feel comfortable and safe to venture beyond the urban areas and beach resorts into the vast tropical rainforests which still cover more than 60% of the land area of Malaysia. The vast potential of our natural heritage has yet to be fully tapped.

It is therefore the government's policy to promote nature and adventure tourism as well as to encourage the conservation of our natural and cultural heritage. Some of Malaysia's most well known natural heritage including Mt. Kinabalu, Niah Caves, Mulu Caves, orang utans, proboscis monkeys and rafflesia flowers are found in Sabah and Sarawak. Indeed, the two states have all the right ingredients for creating a unique tourism product.

I congratulate the author for the timely publication of this book and complementing the government's efforts to promote nature and adventure tourism for Visit Malaysia Year in 1994.

(DATO' SABBARUDDIN CHIK)

# Message of the
## Honourable Minister of Tourism and Environmental Development Sabah

As Sabah prepares to celebrate another Visit Malaysia Year in 1994, it is indeed appropriate that a tourism publication be launched in line with the promotion of nature, adventure and culture tourism.

What Sabah has to offer to the international tourists is not just its rich cultural diversity and its colourful festivals which are celebrated throughout the year. Its natural heritage indeed ranks among the most unique in the world. It ranges from such exotic flora like the rafflesia flower to the abundance of wildlife such as the affectionate orang-utans and proboscis monkeys.

For these reasons, the State Government has placed much emphasis on promoting Sabah as a tourist destination through multi-lingual brochures and videos. In addition, international sporting events are also organised to project Sabah's image.

I congratulate the author for his pioneering effort to promote Borneo as an upcoming ecotourism destination. This publication will indeed serve as a useful guide to individuals and tour companies in updating their product knowledge of Borneo.

I hope the wonderful images in this book will move you personally to visit Borneo too. Happy reading.

(THAM NYIP SHEN)

## Message of the
## Honourable Minister of Environment
## and Tourism
## Sarawak

This book "Journey Through Borneo" will serve to showcase one of Sarawak's main tourism resources and that is, its tropical rainforests with its diversity of fauna and flora and plurality of ethnic cultures.

Sarawak, with its green environment, is the mecca for those seeking adventure amidst a wild and rugged terrain interspersed often by mighty rivers and some of the most spectacular physical wonders to be found on the island of Borneo. The flagship of the State's travel industry, the Mulu Caves, is second to none in the world.

We have all the ingredients for an exciting travel-oriented towards adventure, nature and culture. "Journey Through Borneo", I hope, will also bring you on as exciting a journey through the many sights and wonders of Sarawak as brilliantly captured in photographic form on the pages of this book.

(DATUK AMAR JAMES WONG KIM MIN)

Sunrise over Mt. Kinabalu from Tamparuli.

# CONTENTS

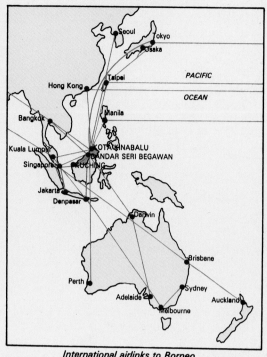

International airlinks to Borneo

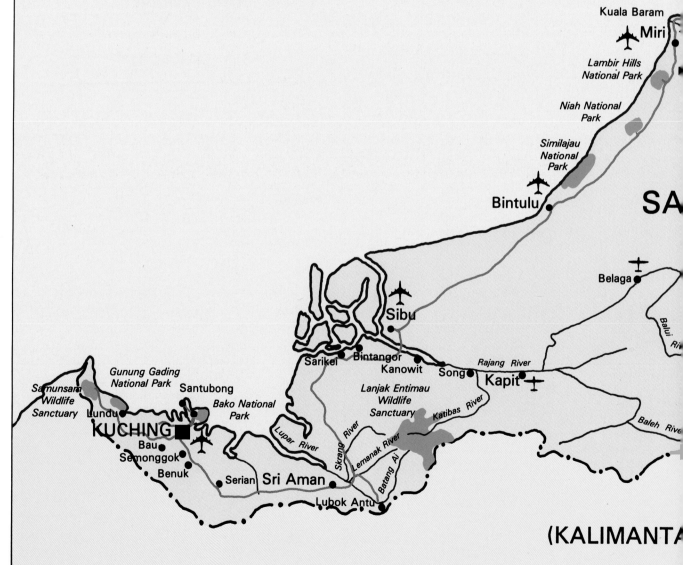

SOUTH CHINA

BANDAR SER

Kuala Baram

✈ Miri

*Lambir Hills
National Park*

*Niah National
Park*

*Similajau
National
Park*

✈
Bintulu

SA

Belaga ✈

✈ Sibu

Sarikei
Bintangor
Kanowit
Song
*Rajang River*
Kapit ✈

*Balui
River*

Samunsam
Wildlife
Sanctuary
Lundu
*Gunung Gading
National Park*
Santubong

*Bako National
Park*

KUCHING ■ ✈
Bau
Semonggok
Benuk
Serian
Sri Aman

*Lupar River*
*Skrang River*
*Lemanak River*
*Batang Ai*
*Lanjak Entimau
Wildlife
Sanctuary*
*Katibas River*

*Baleh River*

Lubok Antu

(KALIMANTA

Gua Kira leading to the Painted Caves in Niah National Park, Sarawak.

It is not certain when human beings first came to Borneo. Evidence shows that Stone Age people may have lived in Peninsular Malaysia as long as 75,000 years ago. These early inhabitants may have spread from mainland Asia south to Australia.

The earliest signs of man's existence in Borneo come from Sarawak, where an Australoid skull and coarse chopping tools dating from an estimated 35,000-40,000 years ago were unearthed in the famous Niah Caves. The south east of Sabah also shows interesting signs of early human habitation. People evidently lived around a large lake, Tingkayu, about 20,000 - 30,000 years ago, moving to limestone caves exposed when the lake later drained away. These people, who produced relatively advanced stone tools, were probably also of Australoid stock, akin to Australian Aborigines. It is not clear why they later died out in Borneo.

It is thought that the forebears of today's ' indigenous' Borneans, such as the Muruts, Kadazans and Dusuns, were people of Mongoloid stock, arriving only 3,000 to 5,000 years ago from the Asian mainland, probably via the Philippines. These early settlers originally lived around the coastal areas of Borneo, but were slowly driven inland by later arrivals, and over the years remained relatively isolated in the interior regions.

Bronze and copper artefacts were being produced between 2,000 and 1,000 years ago, and later, from about 1,000 AD, burial coffins and burial jars were in use, several of which have been discovered in Sabah and elsewhere. Imported goods such as ceramics, glass beads and iron show up as early as 1,300 years ago.

Caves throughout Borneo were undoubtedly places of permanent human habitation until as recently as the 16th century. Borneo contains no remains of large stone temples or ancient cities, as can be found in other parts of South East Asia, as most dwellings were made of wood, which in the tropical heat and humidity decays rapidly and leaves no trace. The only permanent stone buildings dating from pre-European times are in Brunei, including what is thought to be the Sultan's palace or fort at Kota Batu, on the banks of the Brunei River.

Possessing less fertile soils than its neighbours such as Java, Borneo did not attract as many immigrants during this time. The island was also further from the major trade routes and thus experienced less external influence from trade and the spread of new religions. This was especially so in the inaccessible interior regions. Borneo has experienced many internal conflicts throughout its history, however, different tribes often making long-distance overland migrations which not uncommonly precipitated, or were precipitated by, internal wars.

Carving on a belian wood coffin from Batu Tulug, Sabah.

A Spanish map of Borneo from the year 1616. Correct orientation can be obtained by turning the map 90° clockwise.

The huge island of Borneo was strategic however, in so much that it had to be circumnavigated by the European colonising powers of the Spanish, Portuguese, Dutch and English to reach the much sought after spices from the islands of present-day eastern Indonesia. The most common route was from the major port of Malacca down round the tip of Peninsular Malaysia, then up round the north of Borneo. This was largely how the then thriving coastal state of Brunei became known to the West, the first recorded Europeans to visit Brunei being in the early 1500's.

As European exploration pushed ahead in the 16th and 17th centuries, various maps of the area were produced. But it wasn't until 1627, when Pedro Berthelot circumnavigated the island, that the first fairly accurate maps of Borneo emerged. Most depicted a large bay, (Brunei Bay), on the north west coast, labelled as 'Borneo'. The whole island was also called 'Borneo', or variations of it, such as 'Bruneo' and 'Burney'. It thus seems likely that the word Borneo is a Western corruption of the vernacular, 'Brunei'.

The word 'Kalimantan' does not appear on the old European maps, but this ancient local name may mean 'river of precious stones', (diamonds being found in central Borneo); other possibilities are that it comes from the word 'lamanta', the name for the edible starch extracted from wild sago, or that it derives from the name of a type of mango commonly found in Kalimantan; no one is sure.

From as long ago as 700 AD, trade had existed between Borneo and China, and also probably with India and Sumatra. The rainforest provided most of early Borneo's export commodities including camphor, damar (resin from trees and used in Europe in the production of paints, varnish and linoleum), rhino horn, hornbill casques, turtle eggs, birds' feathers, bees' wax, rattan, illipe nuts, scented gaharu wood, bezoar stones and bananas. These items were collected by the indigenous jungle tribes. Later, gold and diamonds were also exported, and possibly not until the 18th century was one of the most famous commodities - edible swiftlets' nests - collected from Borneo's caves and exported for use in the Chinese delicacy, Birds' Nest soup. In return, ceramic wares, metal, cloth and ornaments such as glass beads were imported.

Brunei Bay was the main point of export, with virtually the whole of coastal Borneo coming under the control of the Sultanate of Brunei during the height of its power from the 1300's to the 1700's. From the mid-19th century, European influence, particularly that of the British in the north of Borneo, and the Dutch in the south, increased.

Sarawak was ceded from Brunei in 1841, and later became a British Protectorate, then a colony in 1946. Sabah was known as British North Borneo from 1882 to 1963, being first ruled by the British North Borneo Chartered Company, and after the war becoming a British Crown Colony. Both Sabah and Sarawak gained independence from Britain and joined the Federation of Malaysian States in 1963, whilst Brunei, although a British Protectorate from 1888 to 1984, remained a sovereign state and a Malay Muslim Monarchy.

Today, with a combined human population of only 3.8 million in an area of over 200,000 sq. km, Sabah, Brunei and Sarawak retain much of their natural heritage. The forests of Borneo have been evolving for many millions of years, and during this long period the extent and distribution of different forest types must have varied greatly, influenced by changes in climate and sea levels, and other geological processes. Borneo's rainforests can currently be broadly divided into five groups: mangrove and nipa forest, freshwater swamp forest, dipterocarp forest, heath forest and montane forest.

The most well known are the dipterocarp forests, which occur from just above sea level to about 900 metres. They represent one of the most complex and diverse ecosystems in the natural world. A single 0.5 sq. km plot may contain over 800 tree species, while a comparable area of forest in Europe or North America would contain at most 100 species, and none of the climbing plants and palms. In total, Borneo is reckoned to have a staggering 11,000 species of vascular plants (comprising flowering plants, ferns and their allies), of which most are represented in Sabah and Sarawak.

Borneo's animal life is no less impressive, although much of it well concealed and requires a little time and care to see. Borneo is home to the rare Sumatran Rhinoceros, Clouded Leopard, Asian Elephant, Proboscis Monkey, Orang Utan, Tarsier, Sun Bear, Slow Loris, hornbills, crocodiles, turtles, and much much more.

Add to that the fascinating array of culture, history and people and your Journey Through Borneo will be an experience you will never forget.

Children at the Sabah International Dragon Boat festival.

# Introduction to Sabah

**S**abah, at the northern tip of Borneo, has perhaps the most varied topography of the whole island, including the highest mountain between the Himalayas and New Guinea, probably the best mangrove stands in Malaysia, and some of the most spectacular coral reefs in the world.

At 73,620 sq. km., Sabah is about the same size as Ireland, and is the second largest of Malaysia's thirteen states. Its 1,440 km heavily indented coastline is fringed by three seas: the South China Sea to the west, the Sulu Sea to the north east and the Celebes Sea to the south east. Some 38 islands are dotted around Sabah's coast. The largest tracts of intact mangrove occur on the eastern seaboard, while along the west and northern flanks, long beaches sweep the coast.

And towering over the whole of Sabah is the legendary Mount Kinabalu, a bolt of granite rearing up to a height of over 4,000 metres. This awe-inspiring feature can be seen from many parts of the land, and forms part of the Crocker Range, the backbone of Sabah which stretches from the northern end of the state to the border with Sarawak.

Known as the 'land below the wind' by seafarers who used to seek shelter in Sabah's harbours whilst typhoons raged to the north, this title was immortalised by the writer Agnes Keith, who wrote her novel of the same name whilst living in Sandakan on Sabah's east coast. The name 'Sabah' or 'Saba' is the old Brunei and possibly biblical name, apparently referring to the 'land of the rising sun' or 'land of peace'.

**S**abah's history is infact closely tied in with that of neighbouring Brunei Darussalam, whose control extended over most of coastal Borneo from the 15th to the 18th centuries. The rugged terrain of Sabah's interior however meant that there, the territory effectively consisted of scattered chieftaincies and autonomous communities owing only a nominal allegiance to the Sultans of Brunei.

Trade had existed between the coastal areas of northern Borneo and China since at least 700 AD. Early Chinese records note the existence of a Chinese principality established somewhere along the Kinabatangan River in eastern Sabah. Remains of this settlement have never been found but it is thought that sometime during the 15th century, a marriage took place between either a Chinese princess from the Kinabatangan and the first Sultan of Brunei, or the daughter of the first Sultan of Brunei and a prince from the Kinabatangan, who converted to Islam, and became the second Sultan.

During the late 17th century, internal quarrelling between two of the contenders to the Brunei Sultanate led to one asking for help from the Sultan of Sulu in the southern Philippines. The reward offered was control of the area north of Brunei Bay.... present day Sabah. However this promise was apparently never honoured, and the claim for northern Borneo was disputed by Brunei and Sulu for the next two centuries.

Tombstone of T. B. Harris, part owner of the American Trading Company which began a settlement in Kimanis, south west Sabah, in 1865.

In 1761, the British East India Company signed an agreement with the Sultan of Sulu to begin a trading post on the island of Balambangan, some 20 miles to the north of Kudat, and then in Sulu territory. However 14 years later the settlement was attacked by Suluk pirates and the British driven out. The East India Company had also been ceded a huge piece of northern Borneo stretching from Kimanis north of Brunei Bay, across to the east coast. During this time, when European countries had secured the trading monopolies in most of Borneo, direct trade with China diminished, meaning many local traders lost their means of livelihood. Piracy and slave trading began to increase, causing many people to flee into the interior.

Over one hundred years later, when colonial expansion in South East Asia was at its height, an American trading settlement was established in Kimanis after a 10 year lease had been obtained from the Sultan of Brunei. The settlement failed after a year and in 1875 the lease was sold to the Austrian Baron Von Overbeck. Overbeck obtained financial backing from Alfred Dent in London, and new leases were signed with the Sultans of Brunei and Sulu for an even larger area of northern Borneo.

Chinese lion statue in a Buddhist temple, Kota Kinabalu.

In 1881, all of Dent's rights to North Borneo, including those already transferred from Overbeck, were signed over to the British North Borneo Provisional Association Ltd., which in 1882 became the British North Borneo Chartered Company. Trading posts were established on Gaya Island and in Sandakan, and for two years Kudat became the first capital of North Borneo. Although still ruled by the North Borneo Chartered Company, in 1888 North Borneo also became a British protectorate.

During Chartered Company days, life in North Borneo changed considerably. Piracy and slave trading were reduced, and an extensive system of bridle paths was established, linking previously isolated communities. Tobacco and later rubber were planted to bring in revenue for the Company, and immigration of Chinese farmers was encouraged, to open up farm lands and work in new plantations. The Chartered Company imposed taxes on the native people, precipitating a rebellion led by local hero Mat Salleh, who was related to Bajau and Sulu royalty. In 1897 Salleh and his army looted and razed the British settlement on Gaya Island, and later moved inland building a fort at Tambunan, where Salleh was eventually killed by the British in 1900.

In 1896 work began on the proposed Trans Bornean railway, with construction starting in Weston and Beaufort in south west Sabah. The line progressed to the site that was to become Jesselton, which was established on the mainland after the destruction of the Gaya settlement opposite. The further extensions of the Trans Bornean railway across Sabah to Cowie harbour near Tawau, and to Sandakan, which had replaced Kudat as the capital of North Borneo in 1884, were never completed.

The Chartered Company continued to rule North Borneo until 1946. However the devastating impact of the Japanese occupation from 1942, and the subsequent bombing of the major towns by the Allied Forces at the end of the war, meant that the Chartered Company could not afford to rebuild the shattered infrastructure. Instead North Borneo became a British Crown Colony and in 1946 the capital was transferred from Sandakan to Jesselton on the west coast.

North Borneo, along with the neighbouring British colony of Sarawak, agreed to join the newly formed Federation of Malaysia in 1963, thus gaining independence from Britain. North Borneo regained its pre-colonial name of Sabah and Jesselton was renamed Kota Kinabalu in 1967.

Up until the 19th century, trade from northern Borneo had consisted mainly of jungle products, including high quality camphor and precious cave swiftlets' nests. The rubber estates and tobacco plantations introduced by the Chartered Company in the late 1800's were quite successful for a time, with Sabah producing some of the best grade tobacco leaves in the world.

But in the last 100 years forestry has been the single greatest contributor to the state's economy. Commercial forestry began in 1879, the first timber licence being granted for a concession on Gaya Island, and by 1914 the Forestry Department had been formed by the North Borneo Chartered Company. Log export volumes remained relatively low until the 1950's, and up until this time logging was done by hand axe and cross saw, with the timber being hauled away by manual labour or buffaloes. By the mid 1950's, chain saws and skidder tractors had been introduced, and the 1970's and '80's saw a dramatic increase in timber exploitation, peaking in 1979 when the export of timber products amounted to some 77% of the state's revenue.

Recently, royalties from petroleum from offshore deposits have also contributed substantially to the state's coffers, and as timber resources decline, revenue from other sectors such as tourism will play an increasingly important role. Other notable exports include palm oil and cocoa. Sabah is also home to Malaysia's only copper mine, situated near the foothills of Mount Kinabalu.

A form of the beautiful *Rhododendron javanicum*, found on Mt. Kinabalu.

More than half of Sabah is still forested, with over 40% of the land designated as Forest Reserve, and under the management of the State Forestry Department. Sabah possesses one National Park, and five State Parks, all run by the state government agency Sabah Parks. Three of the Parks comprise off-shore islands and their surrounding waters, while the remainder are mainly forested hills and mountains, including Mount Kinabalu.

Extensive oil palm and cocoa plantations now cover many parts of eastern and southern Sabah, while shifting cultivation and rice growing dominates the west coast and slopes of the Crocker Range.

Sabah's population of over 1.7 million comprises at least 30 different ethnic/linguistic indigenous groups, speaking close to 100 dialects. The majority of Sabah's people are found in the western parts of the state, with a large proportion still living in rural areas.

Dusuns/Kadazans form the major group at around 30% of the population. They are traditionally farmers, inhabiting the west coast from Kudat to the Sarawak border, the valleys of the interior and the slopes of the Crocker Range. Dusuns/Kadazans are a collection of several different groups with distinct languages but similar cultural beliefs, including rice harvest ceremonies and regarding Mount Kinabalu as a resting place of the dead. Many have now been converted to Christianity, whilst a small number have become Muslim and others remain pagan. Dusuns/Kadazans that have settled on the coasts and rivers and converted to Islam, are known as Orang Sungei (people of the river), or Idahans. The Idahan people of Madai near the south east coast of Sabah were already Muslims by about 1400 AD, around the same time as Islam came to Brunei.

Sabah's largest coastal group, the Bajaus, may originally have come from Johor in Peninsular Malaysia, or the southern Philippines. Previously seafaring pirates and fishermen, in the last 100 years those on the west coast settled on the land, while the east coast Bajaus still live largely over, and from, the sea. Other predominantly Muslim coastal groups include the Suluk and Illanun, also from the southern Philippines.

Along with the Dusuns/Kadazans, the Muruts are probably also descendants of the earliest Mongoloid set-tlers in northern Borneo. The Muruts retreated inland, remaining relatively isolated until quite recently, and were Sabah's last ethnic group to stop headhunting. Most are now shifting cultivators, traditionally living in longhouses. Muruts are the third largest indigenous group in Sabah, after the Dusuns/Kadazans and the Bajaus.

The second largest group numerically are the Chinese, who began their immigration to Sabah in the 1880's. The majority are Christian Hakka, emigrating to Sabah originally to work on the plantations, or as farmers. Even today many of Sabah's Chinese are still rural dwellers.

Indonesian labourers, working mostly in the oil palm, cocoa and rubber estates and mainly from Timor, Sulawesi and Flores, along with Filipinos from the southern Philippines, also considerably swell Sabah's population numbers.

Reflecting the wide mixture of ethnic groups in Sabah, religion in the state is both tolerant and diverse. Islam is the official religion as in the rest of Malaysia; however Christianity, Buddhism, Taoism, Hinduism, Sikhism and animism are amongst others also represented.

Administratively, Sabah is divided into five divisions – the West Coast, Sandakan, Tawau, Kudat and Interior Divisions, each headed by a District Officer. The Head of State is the Yang Di-Pertua Negeri Sabah, and presiding over the government is the Chief Minister, backed by a cabinet of nine members. A state general election is held every five years, when the State Legislative Assembly is elected.

The Lotuds and Bajaus of Tuaran and Kota Belud.

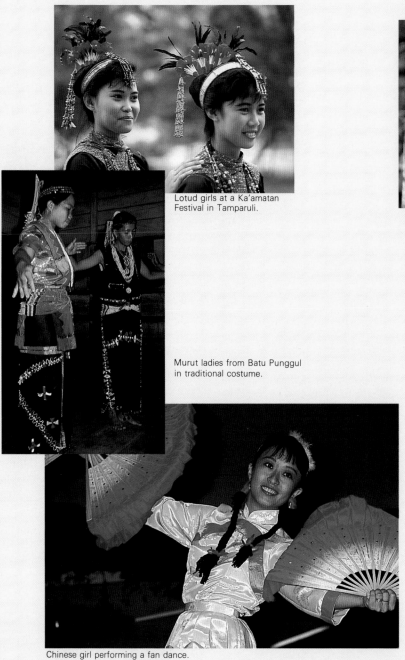

Lotud girls at a Ka'amatan Festival in Tamparuli.

Murut ladies from Batu Punggul in traditional costume.

Chinese girl performing a fan dance.

Bajau horseman in traditional headgear.

Kadazan ladies from Papar at the Ka'amatan Festival celebration.

A Malay kompang troupe at the National Day celebrations.

Just a few of the many different faces making up the fascinating cultural mix that is Sabah. Often the best places to see all the multifarious costumes and dances are at the numerous festivals and celebrations that take place throughout the state, such as the Sabah Fest held every May and preceding the Harvest Festival celebrations, the National Day celebrations in August and the Head of State's birthday parades in September, along with Hari Raya (March/April) and Chinese New Year festivities (January/February).

Almost one hundred years ago, KOTA KINABALU began its history as a replacement settlement for that on Gaya Island opposite, which had been destroyed by local rebel Mat Salleh in 1897. The new settlement was given the name Jesselton, after Sir Charles Jessel, then Vice-Chairman of the British North Borneo Chartered Company.

The first area to be settled on the mainland was around the old wharf, where the present Customs and Excise building is today. This became the terminus of the railway that had begun construction in Weston in 1896. At that time Jesselton was merely a cluster of houses on a narrow strip of land running between the hills and the sea, together with other houses built on stilts over the water. Vestiges of the latter can still be seen in the ever diminishing Kampung Air today. Much land reclamation has occurred since, the first starting around 1900 near the present Hong Kong and Shanghai Bank and godown areas. Areas such as Segama and Sinsuran were reclaimed in 1969.

The original heart of the town centered around the railway line, (with Jesselton Station situated near the Atkinson Clock Tower), and the roads that are now Jalan Tunku Abdul Rahman and Jalan Gaya. Jalan Gaya still boasts some of the oldest shophouses remaining today. The town playing field or 'padang' was in existence as early as 1904.

The development of Jesselton was closely linked with that of the railway, which brought export commodities such as rubber to the deep sea port in the north of the city. Jesselton was also the administrative centre of the West Coast, and continued to flourish until it was virtually flattened during the Second World War. The only pre-war buildings remaining are the old Post Office (now the offices of Sabah Tourism Promotion Corporation) and the Atkinson Clock Tower.

In 1946 Jesselton replaced Sandakan as the capital of Sabah. The town was rebuilt and in 1967 renamed Kota Kinabalu, receiving its status as a Municipality in 1979.

Today Kota Kinabalu (or K.K. as it is affectionately known), is a modern, sprawling town, with an expanding population of well over 200,000.

Kota Kinabalu is continuously growing as more and more land is recla[...]

Atkinson Clock Tower built in 1905, in memory of the town's first District Officer.

sea.

Aerial view of Sabah Museum.

Perched on top of one of Kota Kinabalu's many low hills is the Sabah Museum, the distinctive shape of which is said to mirror a Rungus longhouse. The Museum includes sections on ethnography, archaeology and natural history, as well as a reproduction of a cave showing birds' nests collection, and various life-size traditional houses and an ethnobotanical plant collection in its extensive grounds.

Another old name for Kota Kinabalu, 'Api-Api', literally meaning fire-fire, is still sometimes heard today. This may have originated as the name of a small fisherman's village near Tanjung Aru, and was possibly derived from the local word for a type of mangrove tree, then common in the area, and which attracted many fire flies. It is certain that the name Api-Api predates the burning of the Gaya Island settlement by Mat Salleh, and the various other subsequent fires that occurred in Jesselton.

The capital of Sabah, with its variety of architectura

Kota Kinabalu boasts several other interesting examples of modern architecture, such as the distinctive column-free building housing the headquarters of the Sabah Foundation, a semi-government organisation engaged in commercial, social and educational activities.

Although it is a rapidly developing town, Kota Kinabalu still contains areas of natural beauty like the Likas Bay mangrove stands, and Signal Hill, from where panoramic views of the town and islands can be seen.

A modern office complex, Wisma Tun Fuad Stephens.

The 30-storey Sabah Foundation building commands sweeping views of Likas

The State Mosque, reflecting both contemporary and moorish architecture.

Peak Nam Toong Buddhist Temple.

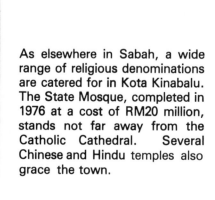

As elsewhere in Sabah, a wide range of religious denominations are catered for in Kota Kinabalu. The State Mosque, completed in 1976 at a cost of RM20 million, stands not far away from the Catholic Cathedral. Several Chinese and Hindu temples also grace the town.

All Saints' Cathedral, built in 1959.

The Gaya Street Sunday Market.

Situated at the end of the long sweeping bay of Tanjung Aru, to the south of Kota Kinabalu, is the beautiful Tanjung Aru Resort. Nearby are the Tanjung Aru race course and the international airport. The railway from Beaufort still terminates in the capital - the main station is now also at Tanjung Aru. Growing along the beach are the distinctive *Casuarina* or 'aru' trees, giving Tanjung Aru its name, and acting as elegant windbrakes along the sandy coast.

The bay provides an excellent mooring for yachts, and also provides a fertile area for crab and mussel collectors, who walk out through the shallows at low tide to the numerous sandbars.

The Sunday morning Gaya Street market is a hive of activity. The road is closed off to traffic and stall holders set up shop, selling everything from antique pottery and brassware to rabbits and plastic buckets. Another veritable treasure trove is the daily Kota Kinabalu central market, where amongst other things luscious jungle fruits, vegetables including asparagus tips from the slopes of Mt. Kinabalu, numerous types of rice and local fresh coffee can be found. Just behind, on the sea front, is the capital's fish market.

Hawkers selling peanuts and local fruits such as rambutans, limes and mangosteens.

The Tanjung Aru Resort is only 15 minutes by boat from the five islands of Tunku Abdul Rahman Park.

Only a few minutes away from Kota Kinabalu lie the islands of TUNKU ABDUL RAHMAN PARK, a haven of peace and tranquility for those who want to get away from it all. Gazetted in 1974, and named after Malaysia's first Prime Minister, the Park comprises five islands, which together with their surrounding waters cover an area of 49 sq. km. Gaya Island is the largest island, and the promontory nearest Kota Kinabalu, where there is a thriving fishing village, is outside the Park boundary. A large part of Gaya Island was gazetted as Sabah's first Forest Reserve in 1923, and remains covered today in a rich coastal dipterocarp forest, now rare in Sabah.

The water village or 'Kampung Air' on Gaya Island, home to several thousand people.

Police Beach in Bulijong Bay, an ideal refuge on Gaya Island.

The mangrove boardwalk on Gaya Island provides a unique opportunity for a relaxed walk through this fascinating habitat.

Day trippers on Mamutik Island, with the mainland in the distance.

The islands' intriguing names can be attributed to the Bajau and Suluk peoples who plied up and down the coast. Mamutik for instance, means a place to collect shells, while Gaya is a corruption of the Bajau word for big. Manukan comes from the Bajau for fish, Sulug is from 'Suluk' and Sapi alludes to the echoes sounding like the mooing of a cow which can be heard on this delightful island.

Chalets on Manukan, popular among locals and tourists alike.

Tunku Abdul Rahman Park is administered by Sabah Parks. Manukan Island is the site of the Park Headquarters, and the most developed of the five islands, with visitor chalets, restaurants, an information centre and other facilities available. Snorkelling gear can be hired on all the islands except Gaya and Sulug, the latter having been left completely undeveloped, for those who want to enjoy the islands in their most natural state.

Fishing with a hook and line is permitted in the Park, but nets and spearguns are strictly prohibited. Sailing and windsurfing are popular, and the islands are a perfect place for picnics and for watching the spectacular sunsets over the South China Sea.

Clean beaches and crystal-clear waters, just two of the priceless assets of Tunku Abdul Rahman Park.

The rainforest and coral reefs of Sapi (left) and Gaya Islands offer excellent possibilities for bird watching, swimming and snorkelling.

View of Sulug Island through the rainforest canopy of Manukan jungle trail.

All the islands except Gaya are covered by old secondary vegeta[tion] most of the original forest long ago cleared by the Bajaus to plant trees and coconut palms. Forest trails on Sapi, Gaya, Manukan Mamutik enable you to explore the interior of the islands. Notice near the beaches are the 'pandan' plants - not palms, but member[s of] the so-called Screw-pine family, the leaves of which are still use[d] making mats, hats and baskets—and the primitive tree-fern-like cyc[ad]

The pineapple-like fruit of the 'pandan', *Pandanus odoratissimus*.

The male cone of the cycad *Cycas nimphii*.

Pied Hornbills are commonly sighted on Sapi and Gaya Islands, especially during fruiting seasons.

The undisturbed forest on Gaya is the richest in wildlife, where occasionally wild boar, and sometimes even pangolin can be seen. More commonly encountered are Long-tailed Macaques, lizards including the large Monitor Lizards which can reach up to 2 metres in length, and numerous butterflies and other insects.

Highlights amongst the birdlife include Pied Hornbills, sometimes glimpsed feeding on fruiting fig trees or flying over Sapi and Gaya, and large flocks of migrant birds such as terns and other waders which visit the islands between September and April.

Sunlight illuminating a boulder coral on the reef.

A delicate feather star gracing the coral reef.

Tunku Abdul Rahman Park is an excellent place to view the underwater world, either through snorkelling or SCUBA diving. Those who don't want to get wet can even take a glass bottomed boat. The coral reefs are best off the sheltered southern and eastern beaches, the western and northern sides of the islands being more exposed and pounded by the swell from the open sea. The complex and fragile ecosystem of the reefs is worthy of respect as well as wonder, and no shells or coral whether alive or dead may be taken from the Park.

A Skunk Clown Fish swimming happily amongst the tentacles of a sea anemone.

Stone megalith in a Penampang rice field.

A Kadazan couple from Penampang district doing the traditional 'Sumazau' dance.

A 'sinningazanak', erected in honour of the owner of a ricefield who died without direct heir

**J**ust outside Kota Kinabalu is the area known as PENAMPANG, a stronghold of Kadazan culture and part of a large rice growing district. In the area stretching south along the coastal plains to Papar, and north as far as Tuaran, solitary megalithic stones can still occasionally be glimpsed standing sentinel in the middle of rice fields. Slightly less widespread are the carved wooden figures or 'sinningazanak'. Both are thought to have been erected by earlier inhabitants as a form of land title. Unfortunately, many have been destroyed as the area has been developed and few remain in situ today. To the Kadazans, rice, and the whole cycle of planting and reaping, are of utmost importance. At 'Kaamatan' or Harvest Festival, which takes place in the month of May, the rice spirit 'Bambaazon' is evoked and thanked for a bountiful harvest. Priestesses play a prominent role in Kadazan religious rituals, as does 'tapai' or rice wine, with much drinking and celebrating in the kampungs.

At TAMPARULI, about 40 minutes drive north of Kota Kinabalu, an impressive suspension bridge hangs across a fast-flowing river. Such bridges are common in Sabah, providing an essential means of communication for local communities, especially in rural areas where roads or concrete bridges may be scarce. Tamparuli Bridge sports metal cables and wire netting, but traditional structures of wood, rattan, rope and bamboo can still be found in the interior.

Tamparuli suspension bridge, one of the longest in Sabah.

The Lotuds are part of the Dusun/Kadazan group, although prefer to be classed under the former, and live mainly around the TUARAN district, not far to the north of Kota Kinabalu. Like the Penampang Kadazans, life traditionally revolves around the growing of rice, and the pagan spirit world. Evil spirits can be exorcised by magic, whilst the large dragon jars, originally brought to Sabah by the Chinese and now of great value, possess spirits which can be extremely friendly. Dances are still performed to the accompaniment of brass gongs, and priestesses chant ancient prayers at time-honoured ceremonies.

The Lotud costumes are predominantly black, with long beaded and brass necklaces worn by the women. Coils of red and black coloured rattan are slung around the hips, as are belts made from old silver coins, similar to other Dusun/Kadazan groups. Famous amongst Lotud handicrafts is the 'Linangkit', the richly embroidered panel tied diagonally across the chest.

Traditional medicine sellers are a not uncommon sight in Sabah's towns, as they set up shop on the pavement or at weekly markets. The various items on offer may include anything from deer's antlers to forest herbs, bark and roots including 'Tongkat Ali', popularly known locally as an aphrodisiac. If the seller is a good showman, crowds will gather round, watching and maybe waiting to be convinced.

Many of the forest plants undoubtedly contain chemicals with medicinal properties, known for centuries to the local people, and now potentially in danger of being forgotten in favour of western medicines, invariably more expensive and themselves often based on forest plant sources. Both local knowledge and the forest plants and their habitat are of great value and should be preserved for future generations.

Equally traditional are the intricate designs in Sabah's Chinese Buddhist and Taoist temples. Incense sticks burn and red colour dominates, with dragons featuring prominently. The Ling San Chinese temple on the outskirts of Tuaran is a fine example of a Taoist worshipping place, and boasts several statues in its grounds, including the formidable Monkey God.

A Lotud high priestess from Tuaran performing a ceremony to appease the spirits of the jars.

Ling San Chinese Temple in Tuaran.

A local medicine man peddling his trade at Tuaran Sunday Market.

Statues from Chinese mythology decorate the temple compound.

Bajau traditional stilted houses over the sea at Mengkabong, with Mt. Kinabalu in the distance

Water village houses and their inhabitants.

About 35 km from Kota Kinabalu, nestling in the coastal mangrove area near the town of Tuaran, is the Bajau water village of MENGKABONG. Here, the houses are built on stilts over the sea, with 'atap' roofs made from nipa palm leaves, and walls made from atap, wood or split bamboo. A network of plankways links the houses with each other and the mainland. While the majority of the west coast Bajaus have settled on the land, these Bajaus, like their cousins on the east coast, are mostly fishermen.

Durians, langsat and tarap fruits, sold by Dusun ladies at the roadside.

A village boy and his dog on their way to sell fruits at a roadside stall in Kota Belud.

**M**arkets are an integral part of local culture and social life, and the market or 'tamu' at KOTA BELUD, less than 2 hours drive north of Kota Kinabalu, is the most famous in Sabah. Every Sunday morning, an area just outside the town is transformed from a relatively tranquil spot to a heaving mass of activity, with people coming from far and wide to sell and buy or just look. Fruits, dried fish, sarongs, handicrafts, hens, cakes, wild honey, tobacco leaves, yeast for making tapai....just about everything can be found here.

'Tudung Saji' or food covers, looking like brightly striped hats, on sale at the Kota Belud Sunday Market.

Cowboys of the east' - the Bajau horsemen from Kota Belud are renowned for their riding skills.

A Bajau woman weaving 'kain darstar', commonly used as headgear on ceremonial occasions by Bajau and Dusuns/Kadazans alike.

Buffalo market at Kota Belud.

When the west coast seafaring Bajaus decided to settle on land in the KOTA BELUD district, about 150 years ago, they took up farming, and buffalo and cattle raising. More surprisingly perhaps, they also became outstanding horsemen.

The horses are in fact ponies, fast and nimble, and are used for transportation and herding livestock. It is thought that they originally came from the stables of the Sultans of Sulu and Brunei, who kept ponies for polo games and as a means of travel.

Many of the ponies are raced at the Tanjung Aru race course, and a pick-up truck with one or more ponies in the back, manes streaming in the wind as the vehicle makes its way along the windy road from Kota Belud to Kota Kinabalu, is a common, if startling, sight.

The horsemen now go on parade every Sunday, in conjunction with the Kota Belud tamu, and also feature in state festivities and other special occasions, both ponies and riders bedecked in colourful costumes edged with bells and gold brocade.

The land Bajaus cultivate wet rice in the fertile valleys and coastal plains, and the view of Mt. Kinabalu from the Kota Belud and Tuaran districts, with the verdant green rice fields in the foreground, is one of Sabah's finest.

Another highlight of the Kota Belud tamu is the buffalo market, where buffaloes are traded for as much as RM1,000 or more, and are auctioned for slaughter, breeding or export to Brunei. Buffaloes remain an important measure of Bajau family wealth, and are still often included in the price of a dowry.

In the Kota Belud and Tuaran districts, buffaloes wallowing in the muddy rice fields or ambling across the roads are an integral part of the landscape.

The mellow scene of Tempasuk plain at the foothills of Mt. Kinabalu, with rice fields, marshes and grasslands.

**B**eyond Tuaran and Kota Belud, about 4 hours drive from Kota Kinabalu, live the Rungus people, in the northern part of Sabah known as the KUDAT Division. The Rungus are a subgroup of the Dusun/Kadazan family, retaining more of their traditional customs than perhaps any other of Sabah's indigenous groups.

Some still live in longhouses, which differ from others in Sabah by having walls that slope outwards towards the roof. There is a common gallery stretching the length of the longhouse, with each family having its own kitchen and sleeping room along the other side of the longhouse. The interior walls are made from bark, while the floor is constructed from split bamboo.

The Rungus weave particularly fine pots and baskets. Distinctive in the costumes are the brass coils, traditionally worn by the women around the neck, fore arms and legs. Nowadays only the oldest ladies still use this form of decoration. Traditional sarongs, black with intricately coloured designs, are handwoven from handgrown cotton. Shells are used to adorn bracelets, and necklaces are made from colourful beads.

Little rainforest remains in the Kudat Division, and the landscape is largely oil palm and coconut plantations and grassland. The Rungus practise shifting cultivation, growing hill rice, maize and tapioca, and a variety of vegetable and orchard crops.

Elaborate beaded necklaces, forming part of the ■

The rare sight of a Rungus lady wearing a brass neck coil.

A modern wedding in a traditional longhouse setting.

Pounding rice to remove the husks.

The busy co■

of a Rungus girl.

ry in a Rungus longhouse.

Rungus girls on the single piece of carved hardwood that forms the steps up to a longhouse.

The Rafflesia Information Centre near Tambunan.

Rafflesia is a parasite, having no leaves, stem or roots; instead it infects the roots of the Tetrastigma vine. After taking up to nine months to develop from a small, cabbage-like bud to its final size, the flower only blooms for a few days, then withers and dies. It is pollinated by flies attracted to the fleshy-looking, and in some cases, odiferous lobes.

Unfortunately Rafflesia are becoming increasingly rare, as land outside protected areas is cleared for logging and shifting cultivation.

**S**abah is home to one of the most famous and bizarre flowers in the world - the giant Rafflesia. About one hour from Kota Kinabalu, 58 km along the scenic road over the CROCKER RANGE to Tambunan, a Forest Reserve has been created specially to protect this fascinating plant. Here an Information Centre introduces you to the biology and conservation problems of Rafflesia, and a walk in the beautiful hill dipterocarp forest of the Reserve may, if you are lucky, reveal one or two specimens in bloom.

At least three of the world's 15 species of Rafflesia are known to occur in Sabah. The largest of all, *Rafflesia arnoldi,* is found in Sumatra and Sarawak, and can grow to an enormous one metre across. The *Rafflesia pricei* found in Sabah's Rafflesia Forest Reserve can reach about 30 cm, almost one foot, in diameter.

A visitor with a *Rafflesia pricei.*

A double bloom of *Rafflesia pricei,* a very rare sight.

The Crocker Range National Park is ideal for jungle trekking.

The Crocker Range is the backbone of Sabah, stretching from the northern end of the state to the Sarawak border, and separating the narrow lowlands of the west coast from the interior of Sabah. To fully appreciate this mountain range, a 5-day trek is recommended, starting at an altitude of about 1,500 metres, and descending to almost sea level, near Penampang.

The trek passes through both montane and lowland dipterocarp forest, affording spectacular views over the countryside along the way. Highlights of the journey include fording clear, rocky rivers, crossing native bridges made from bamboo, and sampling wild fruits in the forest. Nights are spent camping or staying in remote kampungs and chatting with the local inhabitants.

Nature trekkers crossing one of the many crystal clear rivers in the Crocker Range National Park.

Looking back at the hills and valleys of the Crocker Range.

Most of the mountain range is encompassed in the Crocker Range National Park, gazetted in 1984 and Sabah's largest park, at 1,399 sq. km. The highest point in the mountain range is Mt. Alab at 1,964 metres, just outside the National Park boundary. The steep mountain slopes and nearby interior valleys form the water catchment area for much of the west coast.

The trek also passes lush rice fields and bamboo groves.

Clambering up notched bamboo poles strategically placed at difficult sections of the river bank.

Just 2 hours drive inland from Kota Kinabalu is the lush, fertile valley of TAMBUNAN. The road to Tambunan follows the route of an old bridle path over the top of the Crocker Range, then drops dramatically to reveal the Pegalan River winding through the wide valley bottom, and the Trus Madi range of hills on the far side.

Most of the valley's 17,000 or so inhabitants are Dusun/Kadazan rice farmers. Other crops cultivated on the rich, alluvial soil include cocoa, oil palm, rubber, coconut and fruit trees and vegetables.

Buffaloes can be seen everywhere; they still play a central role in Dusun/Kadazan culture and are used to plough the land and haul bamboo from nearby forests. The bamboo has many uses, including for house construction and as pipes to conduct water, for making shelves and fences and as firewood. It is also used for weaving baskets and hats, and the tender bamboo shoots can be eaten. This multi-purpose product of the forest is celebrated every year in Tambunan's Bamboo Festival. Most of Tambunan's Dusuns/Kadazans are now Christians, while some retain animistic beliefs, and there is also a sizeable Muslim community.

More than 70 villages are scattered amongst the valley's broad plains. Wet rice or 'padi sawa' is grown here, giving the valley a glowing, fresh green colour contrasting with the dark green of the hills. The rice seedlings are planted in open water where the ground is flat. This form of rice cultivation has the advantage over dry hill rice in that less weeds can grow in the water. In Tambunan the rice is harvested once a year. Particularly impressive wet rice terraces can be seen at Sinsuron, a village at the head of the valley.

Tambunan is the place where local hero Mat Salleh met his death in 1900, and a memorial plaque marks the site of the fort where he and 300 of his men were killed by the British.

The Kota Kinabalu-Keningau highway runs the length of the valley, and Tambunan provides a scenic stopping point for journeys further into Sabah's interior.

A Dusun lady carryi

The rice fields of Tambunan plain.

r 'wakid', full of bamboo firewood.

A typical country scene in Tambunan.

Coils of forest-collected rattan for sale at the roadside.

The road from Tambunan winds out of the valley, passing Sabah's second highest mountain, MT. TRUS MADI, at 2,642 metres. To reach the peak it is necessary to drive for one hour along logging roads from Tambunan, to the beginning of the summit trail at about 1,525 metres. The summit can be reached by late the same day. One or two nights camping on the summit are recommended to explore the area fully.

Alpine vegetation on Mt. Trus Madi.

The montane forest on Mt. Trus Madi is home to several species of carnivorous pitcher plants, which thrive in the misty, cool environment. The strange-shaped pitchers are in fact elongated leaf tips, which form a funnel or jug-shaped structure. Flies and other insects fall into the pitcher, and, unable to climb up the slippery sides, are digested in the enzyme-rich solution in the bottom, thus supplementing the diet of the pitcher plants which tend to live on nutrient-poor soils.

Nepenthes edwardsiana.

Nepenthes trusmadiensis, endemic to Mt. Trus Madi.

The recently discovered *Rafflesia tengku-adlinii*, which grows in the Trus Madi range.

Summit trail, Mt. Trus Madi.

Mt. Trus Madi offers spectacular views of Mt. Kinabalu to the north; in between lie the valleys of the interior plain. The vegetation on the summit of Mt. Trus Madi was originally stunted moss forest, however this has been cleared and now only shrubs remain. The springy soil is absorbent and peaty, and on the summit ridge, orchids, mosses and epiphytes are common, with at least 11 species of rhododendron blooming on the mountain.

View of Mt. Kinabalu from Mt. Trus Madi.

Tenting on the summit.

*Rhododendron variolosum.*

The sleepy town of TENOM lies in the south west of Sabah, in the heart of Murut country. It is accessible by road via Tambunan and Keningau, a journey of some 3-4 hours from Kota Kinabalu. The road from Tambunan passes through the logged forests of the Keningau plains, Keningau being a thriving timber town and the capital of Sabah's Interior Division. Tenom can also be reached by train from Beaufort.

Tenom is located in one of the major agricultural districts on the west coast, and is the main centre for the coffee and rubber-growing industries. About 60% of the population of Tenom is said to be Murut.

The main attraction in the area is the Agricultural Research Station, with its famous Orchid Centre and Living Crops Museum. The Station was started in 1971 and is situated at Lagud Sebrang, a 20-minute drive from Tenom town. The Orchid Centre has an impressive collection of native orchids and also some hybrids, amounting to over 450 species. Collections of other plant groups such as native gingers, begonias and pitcher plants are also kept at the Centre.

Cocoa tree in Tenom Agricultural Research Station.

Phalaenopsis pantherina.

Ripening coffee berries.

In the Living Crops Museum, over 500 species of crop plants from all over the world can be seen, including tropical fruit trees, vegetables and spices, forming a unique living collection. A resthouse on a nearby hillside offers panoramic views over the Agricultural Research Station and Tenom valley.

The orchid Renanthera bella.

Thrixspermum sp. orchid.

Starfruit *Averrhoa carambola*, also known as carambola or 'belimbing', which grow wild in Indonesia and are widely cultivated in South East Asia.

Just some of the vast array of fruits, both local and foreign, on display in the Living Crops Museum. The fruit, nut and seed trees form one of the largest sections of the collection, and specimens grown include those with enticing and exotic names like the 'scrambled egg fruit tree', and the 'monkey pot' or 'paradise nut tree'.

The Malay apple *Eugenia malaccensis*, related to the guava and native to

A native of Central and South America, the Egg fruit or 'Cannistel' *(Pouteria campechiana)*.

Jakfruits or 'nangka', *(Artocarpus heterophyllus)*, originally from India and now grown fruits, with their large seeds and yellow waxy flesh, can measure up to 100 cm long ar largest cultivated fruit in the world.

Rollinia deliciosa or 'biriba', another of the exotic species found in the Living Crops Museum.

Established in 1988, the Living Crops Museum covers an area of almost three hectares. Within the garden, other sections include mechanised cash crops, leguminous cover and root crops and tree, leafy and fruit vegetables. One of the most interesting collections comprises the spice and condiment plants, where gingers, mint, tumeric, chilli, cloves, nutmeg and cinnamon are amongst examples grown. Further sections feature masticatory crops such as betel nuts and tobacco; beverage and vegetable oil crops; cottage industry crops such as rattan and bamboo; fibre crops; medicinal plants, of which over 140 different types have so far been planted, and insecticidal, perfume and industrial crops.

Guided tours of the Museum are available and specimens are labelled with English, local and scientific names. Increasing awareness of the world's crops, and in particular those fruits which may have potential locally, forms an important part of the work carried out at the Museum, as do research efforts to maintain genetic diversity.

There are plans to develop the site into an Agricultural Park, of which the Orchid Centre and Living Crops Museum will form integral parts.

Berries of the pepper plant *Piper nigrum*, originally from India. The commerial end product of black, white or green pepper depends on how these berries are processed.

From the same family as the jakfruit, breadnut, or 'kamansi' *(Artocarpus camansi)*, can be cooked as young fruit or the seeds deep fried.

he Asian tropics. These huge compound
iameter, making them probably the

*Bulbophyllum sp sect Cirrhopetalum,* one of Sabah's most beautiful orchids which can be seen at the Tenom Orchid Centre.

*Phalaenopsis amabilis,* the 'moth' or 'moon' orchid.

Muruts with a fish trap and basket made from bamboo.

A Murut longhouse at Kampung Tertaluan.

Young Murut girl at Pensiangan.

The Muruts are one of Sabah's interior indigenous peoples, and can be divided into those from the highlands, coming from the area around Pensiangan, and the lowland Muruts living around Tenom. Muruts also inhabit the north-east part of Sarawak.

Longhouse life is now making way for kampung-like individual houses, as are blow pipes for shot guns, used to hunt wild pig, deer and monkey. Rice, maize, sweet potato, sago, sugar cane and fruit trees are amongst crops cultivated. Many families are now involved in rubber tapping.

As with many of Sabah's indigenous groups, the Murut older generations are partial to chewing betel nut and tobacco; and all still enjoy drinking tapai made from fermented rice or tapioca. In the old days tapai was an integral part of celebrations to mark the taking of heads. Many Muruts have now converted to Christianity, however some animist beliefs remain, and like the Dusuns/Kadazans, the lowland Muruts believe their souls migrate to the summit of Mt. Kinabalu.

Murut family, with a charm above the doorway.

A Lundayeh bamboo band.

One interesting feature of some Murut longhouses is the 'lansaran' - a sunken platform on bamboo springs, that bounces up and down like a trampoline, and is used in religious ceremonies and in jumping competitions. One of the few remaining lansarans can be seen at Kemabong, about 24 km south of Tenom.

Most famous of the Murut dances is the breathtaking 'magunatip', where dancers jump nimbly between bamboo poles which are rapidly banged together, risking serious injury to novices' ankles!

Muruts dancing on a 'lansaran'.

The Lundayeh people live in the far south west of Sabah, near the Sarawak and Kalimantan borders, centred on the remote village of Long Pa Sia. An indigenous group similar to the Muruts, although from a different linguistic family, they are well known for their bamboo pipe music.

Climbe

Inland from Tenom, a 3-4 hours drive south of Keningau lies the small village of Sapulut. From here, another 2-5 hours upriver in a longboat will take you to BATU PUNGGUL, a huge limestone massif on the banks of the Sapulut River. Overnight stays can be made in a nearby resthouse or longhouse-style accommodation.

Climbing to the 170-metre summit of Batu Punggul is not easy, but excellent views of the surrounding forest can be obtained from the top. Caves have recently been discovered at Batu Tinahas nearby.

The boat journey itself is interesting, passing rapids and involving clambering out of the boat and pushing it if the water level is low, usually during the months of October to February.

Those who wish to stay longer at Batu Punggul can go fishing or jungle trekking or visit other longhouses along the river. The Murut people who live in this area are famous for their hospitality, and Batu Punggul is as sacred to them as Mt. Kinabalu is to the Dusuns, being the site of various local legends.

Batu Punggul limestone massif towering above the Sapulut River.

kface of Batu Punggul.

The summit of the 170-metre outcrop.

The train and railcar operating between Beaufort and Tenom.

**B**orneo's only passenger trains ply between Tenom and Kota Kinabalu. The narrow-gauge railway runs alongside the fast-flowing PADAS RIVER between Tenom and Beaufort. From Beaufort to the terminus in Tanjung Aru in the capital, the 92-km line passes through transitional and mangrove forest, rice fields and numerous kampungs.

It is possible to hire a 5 or 13-seater railcar — your own personal train — for the journey between Tenom and Beaufort. Regular locomotive trains also operate on this route three times a day.

This historic railway was constructed by the British North Borneo Chartered Company at the turn of the century, originally to open up the interior and facilitate the transport of rubber and other products from the agricultural region around Tenom. It provides an essential and cheap means of communication for many local people, including children going to school and ladies with market produce to sell, and is a unique and pleasant way of viewing Sabah's countryside.

Whitewater rafting on the Padas River.

The Padas River promises some of the best rafting in Borneo. The river carves its way through the Crocker Range on its journey to the west coast, creating the Padas Gorge where dramatic rapids occur. It is possible to take the railcar to a spot on the river from where a 2-hour whitewater rafting trip downstream can be made. After the exhilaration of battling with the powerful river, the railcar is boarded again for the return journey to Beaufort, then to Kota Kinabalu by road, a 90-minute drive.

Adrenalin-pumping moments in the rapids.

PULAU TIGA PARK is located off the south-west coast of Sabah, a 140-km drive south of Kota Kinabalu to the small town of Kuala Penyu, followed by a further short drive and a 45-minute boat ride.

It is one of Sabah's five State Parks and was gazetted in 1978, covering a total area of 158 sq. km. The Park comprises three islands, the largest - Pulau Tiga - housing the Park Headquarters. There is a network of trails around the island, and one resthouse for visitors.

Beach and jetty on Pulau Tiga.

Green Imperial Pigeon.

Scrub fowl on its nest mound of sand and leaves.

Yellow - lipped Sea Krait *Laticauda colubrina* resting on Kalampunian Damit Island.

There are three mud volcanoes on the island, now largely dormant, however every so often bubbles of gas rise to the surface and splatter mud on the trees nearby. Pulau Tiga's three low hills were formed partly by the action of mud volcanoes in the past.

Previously a Forest Reserve, the vegetation on Pulau Tiga is largely undisturbed, with *Barringtonia* trees along the shoreline, and a stand of *Casuarina* covering the hilltop formed by a mud volcano eruption in 1941. Wild fruit trees are common, and there is a small area of mangrove.

Scrub fowl (megapode birds), nightjars, Pied Hornbills and frigate birds can be seen; flying foxes roost behind the mangrove inlet and monitor lizards and Long-tailed Macaques are often encountered. Coral reefs fringe parts of the islands.

The other two much smaller islands, Kalampunian Besar and Kalampunian Damit, lie 20 minutes to the north of Pulau Tiga. Kalampunian Damit is celebrated for its colony of amphibious sea-snakes, the venomous but non-aggressive Yellow-lipped Sea Kraits, which lay their eggs amongst the rocks and crevices on the island.

A 3-metre high mud volcano.

Mt. Kinabalu.

Sunrise over the mountain.

**A**s the dawn light spreads over Sabah, one feature is revealed that dominates all others ... With its jagged outline and massive bulk, MT. KINABALU is a truly imposing sight, held in awe by all that behold it. Indeed this fabled mountain is believed by many Dusun/Kadazan people to be the resting place for the souls of the departed, and is shrouded in superstition.

The origins of the mountain's name are obscure - one theory is that it derives from 'Aki Nabalu', meaning 'revered place of the dead' in local Dusun dialect; another that the name comes from 'Kina-Balu', or 'Chinese widow', relating to a legend involving dragons, a local girl, and a Chinese prince.

What is certain is that Mt. Kinabalu is a botanical paradise, with lowland dipterocarp rainforest, montane forest, cloud forest and alpine meadow vegetation encompassed in the mountain's 4,101 metres (13,455 feet), making it one of the most remarkable plant assemblages in the world.

A tree bathed in sunlight on the mountain.

Mt. Kinabalu is the focal point for Kinabalu State Park, Sabah's oldest park, gazetted in 1964 to include the mountain itself and much forested land to the north. Comprising an area of some 754 sq. km., Kinabalu Park is second only to the Crocker Range National Park in size.

Park Headquarters is situated at the southern boundary of the Park at an altitude of 1,554 metres, and 2 hours drive (90 km) along the Kota Kinabalu - Ranau - Sandakan road.

At this elevation the forest is classed as montane, dominated by oaks and chestnuts. Tree ferns can be seen here, and various species of pitcher plants, which are replaced by different types higher up the mountain.

At about 2,000 metres, the mossy or cloud forest begins, where the trees become stunted and gnarled and where mosses, epiphytes, rhododendrons and orchids abound. There is an abrupt change of vegetation at 2,650 metres, when the conifer *Dacrydium* becomes the dominant tree. The mossy forest returns again later, until the tree line at about 3,350 metres. Above this, shrub-like alpine meadow plants, grasses and sedges are the only things that can survive the cold, bleak environment, along with the white-flowered *Leptospermum* and stunted Heath Rhododendrons.

The first recorded ascent of Mt. Kinabalu was made in 1851 by Sir Hugh Low, then British Colonial Secretary in Labuan. Although his climb did not take him to the actual summit, the mountain's highest peak is named in his honour. It wasn't until 37 years later, in 1888, that the summit was reached by zoologist John Whitehead, who made the ascent with the help of local Dusun porters.

Alexandra Peak
(4,003m)

St. John's Peak
(4,097m)

Victoria Peak
(4,094m)

Low's Peak
(4,101m)

Ugly Sister Peak
(4,032m)

(4,054m)
Donkey Ears

Cauldron Gap

Kinabalu South Peak
(3,933m)

Sayat Sayat Huts
(3,810m)

Panar Laban Rockface

Gunting Lagadan Hut
(3,292m)

Laban Rata Resthouse
(3,261m)

*Mt. Kinabalu*
*Summit Trail*

Borneo's Paradise
*Sabah Malaysia*

Map showing upper part of trail.

Trekkers on the summit trail at about 3,000 metres.

Aerial view of Mt. Kinabalu from the west.

Sayat Sayat from the summit plateau. The effects of heat and cold, wind and rain, still sculpture the rock surface, creating the many faces of the mountain.

Donkey's Ears shrouded in morning clouds.

Mt. Kinabalu is thought to be the youngest non-volcanic mountain in the world, and was formed only around one million years ago, when a huge granite plug forced its way upwards through the Crocker Range. The mountain is still growing at a rate of about 5mm a year. The top of Mt. Kinabalu is the only spot in Malaysia where freezing point is reached, with ice occasionally forming in the rock pool close to the summit. During the last Ice Age most of the summit was covered by ice, glaciers carving out the precipices and peaks and leaving scratches and striations on the rock face. Most dramatically, the summit plateau was split in two by Low's Gully, a yawning chasm over 1.6km deep.

Victoria Peak at dawn.

Kinabalu is a mountain of many moods... and just as the clouds can clear and the sun burn down brightly, so can the mists close in, enveloping everything - rocks, plants and climbers alike, in a cold, grey ethereal world where visibility can be reduced to a few metres.

Bundu Tuhan from the summit plateau.

Rockface above Laban Rata resthouse.

Oyayubi or Thumb Peak.

Low's Gully as viewed from the summit.

Donkey's Ears.

Low's Peak from the West.

Climbers examining an aplite dyke on the summit.

View of Alexandra Peak (4,004 metres), and Oyayubi, West and Dewali Peaks (right)

The first paragliding descent from Mt. Kinabalu by Franz Walch and Till Gottbrath in 1990.

Birds-eye view of Kundasang and Ranau.

Mt. Kinabalu has always attracted the adventurous and daredevil, including such stunts as paragliding and hang-gliding from various peaks, rock-climbing on the many pinnacles and gullies, abseiling and walking backwards to the top!

The more conventional way is to ascend the mountain on foot, following the 8.5 km summit trail, which snakes its way up the south side of the mountain.

Although arduous, anyone who is reasonably fit can attempt the climb, and so far over 200,000 people have made the ascent, including disabled people on crutches, blind people and people carrying babies on their backs. Some of the local Dusuns, accustomed to the steep terrain and the altitude, can run up and down in less than 3 hours. However, the normal time taken to scale the mountain is 2 days.

Rock climbing on Donkey's Ears.

From Park Headquarters, a 5-km road leads to the Timpohon Gate, start of the summit trail proper, at 1,830 metres. From here, a well-marked trail climbs ever upwards over gnarled tree roots and later rocky boulders, to the resthouses at Panar Laban at 3,350 metres. Visitors normally reach this altitude by early afternoon. After resting and spending the night here, a 3 a.m. start is made the next day to climb to Low's Peak, with the aid of torchlight, and support ropes and ladders over the steeper parts of the rock face. The summit is reached in time for the dawn, which can be seen illuminating large tracts of Sabah stretching out below. After clambering down to Panar Laban, the descent down through the forest takes about 4-7 hours, with most people arriving back at Park Headquarters in the afternoon.

The weather on the mountain can change quickly. Park regulations require that all climbers to the summit must be accompanied by a guide. Porters can be hired to carry backpacks.

Indigo Flycatcher.

Frogs *(Polypedates leucomystax)* mating.

Slow Loris *(Nycticebus coucang).*

Female trilobite beetles.

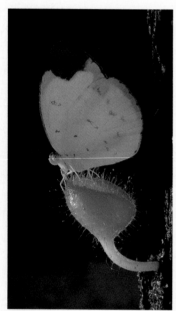
*Eurema* sp. butterfly on a cup fungus.

Although less conspicuous than the flora, Mt. Kinabalu's animal life is very diverse, and comprises over 300 species of bird, and more than 100 species of mammals, the most noticeable being the tree shrews and squirrels, common on the lower trails. Invertebrates abound, including an exceptionally high number of stick insect species.

Rhinoceros beetle.

Rajah Brooke's Birdwing Butterfly *Trogonoptera brookiana.*

Rothschild's Slipper Orchid *Paphiopedilum rothschildianum.*

The orchid *Coelogyne rhabdobulbon.*

*Nepenthes rajah,* the largest pitcher plant in the world.

The mountain and its lower slopes contain an estimated 1,000 species of orchid, at least 26 species of rhododendron and 9 types of pitcher plants, a greater variety than anywhere else on the planet.

Other interesting plants include wild raspberries, wild cinnamon trees, over 40 species of oak, and *Dawsonia,* the largest moss in the world.

The epiphytic Birds' Nest Fern.

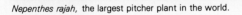

*Rhododendron crassifolium,* on Mt. Kinabalu.

Twin-bed cabins at Kinabalu Park Headquarters.

Kinabalu Park offers a variety of accommodation at Park Headquarters, including chalets, twin-bed cabins and hostels with dormitory beds. Two restaurants are available and there is an exhibit centre where visitors can see displays on the Park's wildlife and ecology. A montane garden brings together many of the Park's most interesting flora, well-labelled and laid out near the Park Administration building.

An extensive network of trails exists in the vicinity of Park Headquarters, and guided nature walks are given every morning by Park Naturalists, along with regular evening slide shows. Bird watching is popular around Park Headquarters, with the Grey Drongo and Malaysian Tree Pie two of the most noticeable avian species.

Up at Panar Laban at 3,350 metres, accommodation is provided for climbers in the form of Laban Rata - a resthouse with electricity, a canteen, hot water and room heaters, and three other huts with more basic facilities.

Panar Laban is a corruption of the Dusun for 'place of sacrifice', and is near where the local guides of the first explorers stopped to appease the souls of their ancestors, before climbing into the spirit world on the summit. A sacrifice of a white cockerel and seven eggs is still made here once a year.

For day-visitors who just want to enjoy the cool and refreshing air and relax around Park Headquarters, or for those who wish to venture up the mountain, Kinabalu Park is ideal.

Laban Rata resthouse at 3,350 metres.

Still inside Kinabalu Park, some 43 km to the east of Park Headquarters, are PORING HOT SPRINGS, accessible by road from the town of Ranau. Poring lies in lowland dipterocarp forest, at the eastern boundary of the Park, at an altitude of 480 metres. It is possible to visit in a day from Kota Kinabalu, although visitors wishing to stay overnight can be accommodated in hostels, cabins or in the camping area near the hot springs.

Not far from the entrance to Poring, over a hanging bridge across the Mamut River, a series of tiled tubs have been constructed where hot sulphur water is piped from a bubbling spring. What more perfect way to soak away the aches and pains and recuperate after climbing Mt. Kinabalu! There is also a refreshing cold water swimming pool nearby.

Around Poring are lush bamboo groves, 'Poring' being the local name for one of the larger species of bamboo, used in the construction of houses and water pipes. Rattan palms with their spiny stems are also abundant. There are several beautiful waterfalls along the trails, and a small group of bat caves about 30 minutes walk from the hot springs.

In contrast to the montane and cloud forests of the higher altitudes of Mt. Kinabalu, the lowland forests of Poring contain many lianas and fruit trees, contributing to the greater number of primates such as Orang Utans and Red Leaf Monkeys, which are sometimes glimpsed along the quieter trails. The bird life is also rich, and numerous colourful butterflies can be seen flitting around the hot springs, attracted by the mineral rich water and the flowering shrubs.

Kipungit waterfall at Poring.

The treetop canopy walkway at Poring.

Twenty minutes along a trail from the hot springs at Poring, a special walkway has been constructed way up in the tree tops, 60 metres above the ground at its highest point. A whole new world of the rainforest canopy is opened up, along with superb birds' eye views across the surrounding forest. For those with a head for heights, this is an experience not to be missed.

In the depths of the lowland forest around Poring is the rare *Rafflesia keithii*, the flower of which can reach over 80 cm across, and has numerous warts on its five fleshy lobes. The smaller *Rafflesia pricei* is also found in Kinabalu Park, but prefers altitudes of 1,200-1,400 metres. To witness a Rafflesia flower is a lucky event, because after blooming for just a few days, the flower blackens and rots away.

As a parasite, Rafflesia is also vulnerable when its host, the *Tetrastigma* vine, is disturbed. Rafflesia cannot be domesticated, translocated, or bred artificially, making the preservation of its natural habitat essential.

*Rafflesia keithii,* found in the rainforest around Poring.

**D**usun/Kadazan people still live on the lower slopes of Mt. Kinabalu, around the Park boundaries. Traditionally shifting cultivators, rice, tapioca, sweet potatoes, sugar cane and tobacco were grown, but more recently permanent terraced farm plots have also sprung up, and temperate vegetables like asparagus, cabbage and lettuce are now also cultivated. Several of the local Dusuns work as rangers and guides in the Park.

Fruits and vegetables are brought to roadside stalls, and 'tamus' or markets, in nearby KUNDASANG and Ranau. These are good places to stop and buy pineapples, bananas of all varieties, and langsat or duku, tarap and soursop when in season. The produce is often carried to the markets in distinctive bamboo baskets or 'wakids'. Cattle farms and a tea plantation can also be seen at this altitude, between Park Headquarters and Ranau.

A Dusun village nestling in the foothills of Mt. Kinabalu.

Vegetable farms near Kundasang.

Roadside fruit stall at Pekan Nabalu, not far from Kinabalu Park Headquarters.

About 20 km from Kinabalu Park Head-quarters, is the Australian War Memorial at RANAU. The Memorial commemorates the so-called 'Death March' of 1944, when the Japanese marched 2,400 Australian and British Prisoners of War from Sandakan to Ranau, a distance of some 240 km. The march took 11 months and only 6 men sur-vived the harrowing journey through the jungle, many succumbing to malaria and other diseases along the way. The Japanese formally surrendered just after – in September 1945 - when North Borneo was liberated by the 9th Division Australian Im-perial Forces. The Memorial was erected by the Australian Returned Soldiers League,

alongside another built to commemorate the local people who also died.

Nearer Park Headquarters, not far from the main road, lie the Kundasang War Memorial display gardens, where flowers and shrubs from Britain, Australia and Borneo are planted.

The town of Ranau is the jumping off point for Poring Hot Springs, 19 km away, and Mamut Copper Mine, the tailing dam of which can be seen along the Poring road. Ranau is also a transit point for buses travell-ing across Sabah to Sandakan on the east coast.

The Australian War Memorial in Ranau.

**S**ANDAKAN is Sabah's premier town on the east coast, and fast gaining a reputation as the gateway to Sabah's richest wildlife areas. It has a population of over 125,000 and is linked to Kota Kinabalu by regular flights, and by road, a 5-8 hour journey.

Sandakan has an interesting history, although sadly little evidence of this remains as the town was demolished during the Second World War. In 1878 William Pryer was installed as the first Resident of the area. Sandakan Bay was already used by the seafaring Suluks and Bajaus, and well known as a fine harbour and as a port of trade for jungle products such as birds' nests, camphor, rattan and sea pearls. Pryer resided first at Kampung German, a village used by European gun runners, then moved to Buli Sim Sim on the north side of Sandakan Bay. The new settlement was originally called Elopura or 'beautiful city', but this soon reverted to the old Sulu name Sandakan, meaning 'place that was pawned'. Timber was first exported in 1885. Trade continued to flourish and in the 1960's and 70's, Sandakan was to become a major timber town with one of the largest numbers of timber millionaires in the world. To this day, log ponds containing valuable timber species can still be seen lining Sandakan harbour.

Chosen as the capital by the British North Borneo Chartered Company in 1884, this honour was transferred to less devastated Jesselton on the west coast after the Second World War.

Sandakan town, with Sandakan Bay behind.

Japanese graves.

Chinese cemetery.

Berhala Island.

Just outside Sandakan Bay is the island of Berhala, with its distinctive rose-orange coloured sandstone cliffs at the southern end. It is here that many of the European Prisoners of War were detained by the Japanese in the Second World War. The island and its beaches are popular weekend haunts of the town people, and easily accessible by boat.

The Puu Jih Shih Buddhist Temple on the hillside above Tanah Merah, a short drive from the town centre, offers unrivalled views over Sandakan Bay. Extensive mangrove stands fringe most of the bay, providing a nursery for fish and prawn populations and making Sandakan the largest and most important fishing port in Sabah.

In the hills at the back of Sandakan, overlooking the Sulu Sea, stands a large Chinese cemetery and a memorial to Japanese soldiers who died during the Second World War, along with the graves of a number of Japanese girls, brought to Sandakan in the early years of the colony and victims of a prostitution racket.

Puu Jih Shih Chinese Temple, completed in 1987.

Within Sandakan town are several places of interest, including the reconstructed house of Agnes Keith, the American writer who lived in Sandakan in the 1930's and 40's, and which stands on a leafy hillside a few minutes drive out of town.

Sandakan is famous of its seafood, and boasts the largest fish market in Sabah, situated next to the fruit and vegetable market right on the seafront.

Also worth visiting is the State Forestry Department Headquarters, 8 km along the Labuk Road. The headquarters houses a museum which is open to the public and includes displays on the history of forestry, and different forest types and forest products.

A little further out on the same road is Sabah's only licensed crocodile farm, containing some 1,200 animals of various ages, bred for their skin and meat.

The tropical setting of the Sandakan Renaissance Hotel.

Lowland rainforest canopy.

A beautifully marked lizard on the forest floor.

Baby Pig-tailed Macaque *(Macaca nemestrina).*

**J**ust 25 km west of Sandakan town lies SEPILOK FOREST RESERVE, an area of some 43 sq. km. of lowland dipterocarp forest and mangrove. The Reserve was gazetted in 1957, and is also the location of the Sepilok Orang Utan Rehabilitation Centre.

The word 'dipterocarp' comes from the name of the dominant family of large trees in this type of forest — the *Dipterocarpaceae*, and literally means two-winged seed. The dipterocarps include the most sought after timber species, with their long straight trunks, many having substantial buttresses at the base. Magnificent specimens of the famous Borneo 'ironwood' or 'belian' can also be seen in Sepilok Forest Reserve.

Mengaris tree *(Koompassia excelsa)* with honeycombs on the branches.

The soaring, straight trunk characteristic of dipterocarp trees.

A variety of wildlife occurs in Sepilok Reserve, including mouse deer, Moonrats, flying squirrels and tarsier. Lowland forest birds are also well represented. Short trails exist around the entrance to the Reserve at the Orang Utan Rehabilitation Centre, and there is a 3-hour walk through the forest to the mangroves abutting Sandakan Bay.

Bornean Gibbon *(Hylobates muelleri)* in Sepilok.

A young Orang Utan *(Pongo pygmaeus)*

One of Sabah's most famous attractions is the world-renowned SEPILOK ORANG UTAN REHABILITATION CENTRE, located on the edge of Sepilok Forest Reserve. The Centre is easily accessible from nearby Sandakan - a mere 20 minutes drive or bus ride away.

Wildlife Department Rangers escort visitors and look after the Orang Utans and other animals at the Centre. Facilities include a visitor reception centre, gift shop and nature education building, where video shows about Orang Utans and the work of the Centre can be seen along with exhibits on Sepilok's other fauna and flora and the ecology of the rainforest.

Adult male Orang Utan.

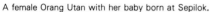
A female Orang Utan with her baby born at Sepilok.

Sepilok Orang Utan Rehabilitation Centre was set up in 1964 by the then Game Branch of the Forestry Department, to deal with the large number of Orang Utans which were being kept in illegal captivity. The Orang Utans, often young individuals whose mothers had been killed, were confiscated from their owners and brought to the Centre for rehabilitation - training in how to live a natural life and reintroduction to the forest. More recently, loss of forest habitat has become the greatest threat to the Orang Utans, and many are brought in from areas cleared for agriculture.

Juvenile Orang Utans learning to survive in their natural habitat.

To-date over 200 Orang Utans have been admitted to the Centre. Some disappear into the Forest Reserve to lead fully independent lives; others reappear occasionally at the Centre, perhaps to supplement their diets in the wild.

The process of rehabilitation involves a period of quarantine for Orang Utans newly admitted, then a daily introduction to the forest to learn skills such as climbing, which if the Orang Utan was very young when it was orphaned, it will not have had chance to learn from its mother.   Once the Orang Utans are more confident, they are released to range where they like, but most stay around the Centre for a while, and visitors can observe their twice-daily feeding sessions when bananas and milk are provided at a platform a few minutes walk from the Centre.

Further into the forest, about 20 minutes walk along a trail, another feeding area exists where a controlled number of visitors can usually see wild or fully rehabilitated Orang Utans come swinging in from the forest for their morning feed.  The arrival of the Orang Utans here cannot be guaranteed.

An Orang Utan building a nest high in the tree tops.

Feeding time at Sepilok.

In order to avoid the spread of disease from Man to the Orang Utans, visitors are not encouraged to touch the Orang Utans, although there may be one or two individuals at the Centre which can be held.

Visitors can explore the forest trails near the Centre without a guide, but it should be remembered that Orang Utans are highly intelligent, often inquisitive animals, and should be treated with the greatest respect.

Play time between an Orang Utan and a Pig-tailed Macaque.

The Sumatran or Asian Two-horned Rhinoceros *(Dicerorhinus sumatrensis)*.

One of the Sumatran Rhinos at Sepilok.

Sepilok is also home to the rare and highly endangered Sumatran Rhinoceros, the smallest, and hairiest, of the world's five species of rhino. Once widespread throughout South East Asia, and even seen wandering on the outskirts of Sandakan town as recently as the turn of the century, the Sumatran Rhino is now reduced to a world population thought to be less than 1,000, with perhaps as few as 50 remaining in Sabah.

Those in Sepilok are individuals which have been rescued from isolated pockets of forest, and which it is hoped will breed in captivity. Other such rhinos may be transferred to the safety of a large wildlife reserve in the south east of Sabah.

The principal reason for the Sumatran Rhino's decline has been poaching, with their horns being illegally traded as a substance believed by some to have medicinal properties; loss of forest habitat is another factor contributing to their decrease in numbers.

Other residents of the Centre at any one time may include Sun Bears, Bornean Gibbons and Proboscis Monkeys, all victims of illegal captivity, destruction of their forest homes, or loss of their family group, and destined for reintroduction to the wild.

Baby elephants are sometimes also brought in - usually orphans which have been rescued from agricultural plantations. These may be trained up for eventual use in elephant control activities in the State.

Turtle tracks on Selingan Island.

Starting young on ed

S ome 40 km north east of Sandakan, in the Sulu Sea and close to the border with the Philippines, lie three small islands known as TURTLE ISLANDS PARK. This is Sabah's third marine park, which, including the surrounding waters and coral reefs, covers an area of 17.4 sq. km.

The three islands, Gulisan, Bakkungan Kecil and Selingan, constitute one of the most important breeding areas for sea turtles in the whole of South East Asia.  First protected in 1971 due to the over exploitation of turtle eggs, which had been collected for generations by local fishermen, the islands became a State Park in 1977.

The Park can be reached in one hour by speedboat from Sandakan, and three visitor chalets are available on Selingan Island, where there is a restaurant and a small exhibition centre.

A female Green Turtle (Chelonia mydas).

Turtle eggs being deposited in the nest hole.

Overnight visitors to Selingan can have the privilege of experiencing the rare and moving spectacle of female turtles coming up on the beach at night to lay their eggs. The majority are Green Turtles, while about 17% are Hawksbills. Visitors are virtually guaranteed a sighting, as both nest throughout the year, with the peak period for Green Turtles between August and October, and for Hawksbills from February to April.

Malaysia's sea turtles are protected species and, as they are easily disturbed by lights and noise, turtle watching is supervised by the Park Rangers stationed on the island.

After digging a large hole in the sand with her hind flippers, the female turtle will deposit an average of about 100 eggs, then cover them with sand and return labouriously to the sea. The whole process may take several hours and during this time the female may often stop to rest.

All the nests are then dug out by the Park Rangers and the eggs carefully counted and transferred to the turtle hatchery, where, some 7 or 8 weeks later, the hatchlings will emerge from the sand, usually at night.

Turtle hatchlings are gathered each night from the nursery.

Visitors can assist the Rangers in releasing the hatchlings on the beach near the water's edge, witnessing the beginning of their life at sea.

Most will fall prey to natural predators, or other causes of death, but some may return, perhaps 20 or 30 years later, to lay their eggs on the very same beach at Selingan.

Turtle hatchlings being released to the sea.

A baby Green Turtle, a mere 8 cm long.

About 2 hours drive from Sandakan, or a 45-minute boat ride across Sandakan Bay followed by a short drive through oil palm plantations, lie GOMANTONG CAVES, a large limestone outcrop and cave system, surrounded by logged lowland forest.

Near to the resthouse and picnic area is the Simud Hitam Cave, where visitors can see the cave swiftlets that produce the so-called 'black' nests, made from hardened saliva mixed with feathers.

Further away is the Simud Puteh Cave complex, home to a different species of swiftlet which produces the more valuable 'white' nests, made of pure saliva. The cave roofs soar up to 90 metres high, whilst on the cave floor thousands of insects teem in the rich guano.

Harvesting birds' nests high up in the cave roof.

The 30-metre high entrance to Simud Hitam Cave.

Local collectors use long rattan ladders and bamboo poles to reach the nests, a perilous but lucrative activity, with the white nests fetching up to US$500 per kg. Harvesting is only allowed during certain seasons, and is controlled by the State Wildlife Department. The nests are both exported and used locally in the Chinese delicacy Birds' Nests soup.

The cave swiftlets share their home with an estimated 2 million bats, whilst outside the caves, birdlife and butterflies are particularly abundant.

Newly-born Mossy-nest Swiftlet.

Edible nest of the White-nest Swiftlet *Aerodramus fuciphagus.*

Gomantong Caves, home to four species of swiftlets.

Lesser Woolly Horsehoe Bat, from forests around Gomantong Caves.

Rattan ladders and ropes suspended from the roof of Simud Hitam Cave.

Mother and baby Proboscis Monkeys.

Male Proboscis Monkey *(Nasalis larvatus)*

Long-tailed Macaque *(Macaca fascicularis)*.

Monitor lizard *(Varanus salvator)*, lounging above a tributary of the

**S**outh of Sandakan Bay, the largest river in Sabah, the mighty KINABATANGAN, flows into the Sulu Sea. It is possible to reach the Kinabatangan River by a 2-3 hour drive from Sandakan, arriving at Sukau village on the banks on the river, or by taking a boat from Sandakan across the bay to Suan Lamba, followed by an hour's drive through an oil palm plantation. From Sukau it is a short trip to Sukau Rainforest Lodge, where visitors can stay overnight.

Late afternoon and early morning are the best times for viewing wildlife, and boat trips are made from the lodge through the tributaries and scattered ox-box lakes of the swamp forest bordering the river itself.

This flat, lowland area on the east coast of Sabah contains a remarkably rich assemblage of wildlife, the most famous denizen of all being the bizarre Proboscis Monkey, endemic to the island of Borneo.

This unlikely animal, with its surprisingly thick orange and grey fur, long pendulous tail and large pot belly, inhabits the riverine vegetation, congregating in trees along the river banks in the late afternoon, always spending the night near the water. Before settling down to sleep, the males can often be seen leaping about and crashing through the trees, competing with other males and defending their female harems. Unlike most other primates, Proboscis Monkeys are good swimmers and have partially-webbed back feet.

Proboscis Monkeys are vegetarian, existing on a diet consisting mainly of leaves and young shoots. The males have enormous drooping noses, which enhance their resonant 'honking' calls, thought to attract females.

Reddish Scops Owl *(Otus rufescens)*.

The swamp forest, although not as tall or diverse as the dipterocarp forest further inland, is very productive of leaves and fruits, and supports abundant wildlife. Other mammals occurring in the area include macaques, leaf monkeys, Bearded Pigs, the rare banteng or 'tembadau', and probably the greatest concentration of Orang Utans and elephants in the whole of Malaysia. Estuarine Crocodiles, once fairly common in Sabah's rivers, including the Kinabatangan, are today rarely seen.

Periodic flooding occurs along the lower Kinabatangan, and the area is permanently waterlogged. The river has long been a highway for jungle produce, and visitors may witness large rafts of logs being towed down to the coastal towns.

Further down towards the mouth of the Kinabatangan River, lush mangrove forests dominate the vegetation. Here mudskippers, crabs and molluscs abound.

Common Night Heron.

Black-throated Babbler.

The swamp forest on the lower Kinabatangan is an excellent spot for viewing birds, particularly water birds such as egrets, herons, storks and the rare Oriental Darter or Snakebird, which dives under water to catch fish.

River.

Rhinoceros Hornbill *(Buceros rhinoceros)*.

Oe of the best places to see unspoilt lowland tropical rainforest is in the remote and beautiful DANUM VALLEY, near the town of Lahad Datu in the south east of Sabah.

The interesting 2-hour drive into Danum from Lahad Datu passes through forest which was logged some time ago, and is in various stages of regeneration. There are some spectacular vistas along the winding road, and particularly striking are the soaring 'mengaris' trees, with their luminous pale grey trunks. Mengaris (*Koompassia excelsa*) are the tallest trees in Sabah, and have been known to reach heights of over 80 metres.

The 92-km journey finally ends at a jungle lodge situated beside the Danum River and on the edge of the Danum Valley Conservation Area, 438 sq. km of lowland rainforest which is being preserved in its pristine state.

Visitors to the jungle lodge can enjoy guided walks with experienced naturalists through both riverine and dipterocarp forest habitats. Activities also include bird watching, mammal spotting on night drives, line fishing in the Danum River and wildlife photography. The lodge provides a perfect setting for relaxing in natural and peaceful surroundings.

Accommodation consists of comfortable traditional-style chalets, and a central building housing a dining area, bar, meeting room with audio-visual facilities and library with display and interpretive materials. The lodge buildings have been designed to blend in with the surroundings and constructed out of local materials, including core-logs from a local plywood factory and river stones.

Near the jungle lodge, a suspension foot-bridge has been built across the Danum River, allowing access to several trails. A viewing platform near a 200-metre escarpment overlooking the lodge gives panoramic views of the river and unspoilt forest in the Danum Valley Conservation Area.

An ancient Dusun burial site was recently discovered at the base of the escarpment, complete with carved belian coffins and ceramic jars. The coffins can be reached by a 45-minute walk up a steep trail from the Danum River. Several attractive waterfalls and rock pools are also found in this area, offering inviting opportunities for a refreshing swim.

Stairway to heaven .....aluminium ladder leading to the 40-metre high ca

Belian coffin

One of the beautiful waterfalls near the jungle lodge.

An hour's drive away is Danum Valley Field Centre, one of the foremost research and environmental education establishments in South East Asia. Research carried out by field scientists based at the Centre has revealed Danum Valley to be an area of outstanding wildlife value, with the elusive Clouded Leopard, Orang Utan, Proboscis Monkey, Asian Elephant and the extremely rare Sumatran Rhino all being found there. Over 270 species of bird have also been recorded, including the rare Bulwer's Pheasant. The flora is no less rich and plants collected have\ included ferns, palms, dipterocarps, orchids, lichens, fruit trees and medicinal plants.

Hikers exploring the Segama River.

At the Field Centre, research facilities include two easily accessible 10-metre high observation towers, and a 40-metre high viewing platform for the adventurous, affording superb views over the rainforest canopy and built next to a magnificent strangling fig tree.

An Information Centre provides displays and detailed maps of the area, and there are a number of forest trails catering for visitors of varying levels of stamina and experience, including two short, well-marked self-guided nature trails with over 300 labelled trees, and more strenuous routes such as the evocatively named Rhino Ridge Trail.

Maiden-veil or Stinkhorn fungus sometimes seen in Danum Valley.

on platform.

Nursery with dipterocarp seedlings.

It is also possible to visit nearby logging, reforestation and research areas, including nurseries where native tree seedlings are being grown for enrichment planting, and sites where reduced impact logging techniques are being tried out. The main objective of both these initiatives is to increase the amount of forest available to absorb carbon dioxide, one of the so-called greenhouse gases.

Danum Valley Field Centre, on the edge of the Segama River and the Danum Valley Conservation Area.

**A** couple of hours drive through oil palm, cocoa and coconut plantations from either Lahad Datu or Tawau brings you to the coastal town of SEMPORNA, inhabited mainly by Bajaus and Suluks, many of whom are fishermen. Some Bajaus still live in traditional house boats or 'lipa'; others inhabit temporary stilted villages perched on shallow sandbars way out in the middle of the sea. From Semporna boat trips can be made to the surrounding islands and coral reefs, most of which have recently been incorporated into a protected island park.

The 'floating' Semporna Ocean Tourism Centre.

An indigenous girl in Suluk costume.

Semporna fish market.

Semporna is recommended for its fresh sea food, including a variety of fish, prawns, crabs and lobsters.

Fisherman with red snapper.

Fresh seafood market.

Sipadan Island, in the Celebes Sea.

**S**emporna is the main starting-off point for the 45-minute speedboat trip to SIPADAN ISLAND, renowned as one of the best diving locations in the world. Sipadan can also be reached by boat or helicopter from the large town of Tawau, further south west along the coast.

Lying in the Celebes Sea, off the continental shelf, Sipadan is the only truly oceanic island in Malaysian waters, rising from the ocean bed as a limestone-capped volcanic sea-mount, topped by a triangular-shaped reef which fans out around the 12-hectare low-lying island.

Accommodation is provided by several diving operators based on the island, who offer a variety of activities including beach, boat and night dives.

Visibility in the warm seas around Sipadan can reach up to 50 metres, and various dive sites with names such as Hanging Gardens, Lobster Lair and Barracuda Point lure visitors. However the *piece de resistance* is the 'drop off' - a sheer reef wall plummeting 600 metres down to the ocean bed, only paces from the beach at one end of the island and marked by the water colour changing dramatically to a deep indigo blue. The wall diving here is world class.

Another unusual dive is to Turtle Cavern, where complete skeletons of stranded turtles lie at the back of a cave in the reef wall. Sipadan has been called the 'turtle capital of the diving world', with Green and to a lesser extent Hawksbill turtles seen in profusion. It is also possible to accompany the Wildlife Department rangers stationed on the island and watch turtles nesting on the beach at night.

Cave diving at Sipadan - the entrance to Turtle Cavern.

Spotted Sweet-lips.

The abundant fishlife around Sipadan includes schooling Barracuda, White-tipped Sharks, Jaks and Bumphead Parrot Fish to name but a few. Because of the great depths, pelagic fish such as large tuna, and occasionally Whale Sharks and Manta Rays, also visit the area. On the reefs, the tunicates, sponges and sea fans are exceptionally rich.

A narrow coral sand beach encircles the island, which is covered by largely undisturbed primary forest fringed by well-developed beach vegetation. Sipadan was declared a bird sanctuary in 1933, and Megapode birds and rare Nicobar Pigeons nest here; the world's largest terrestrial crab, the Robber or Coconut Crab, can also be seen. Fishing is not encouraged around Sipadan, and it is probable the wildlife, reefs and island will be given further protected status in the near future.

Snorkeler at the 600-metre drop-off.

Sunset over Sipadan Island jetty.

Turtle and diver sharing the sea at Sipadan.

Feather star on the vertical reef wall.

**T**he island of LABUAN, off the south west coast of Sabah in the South China Sea, and 123km from Kota Kinabalu, is accessible both by air and by sea. It is a 2-hour ferry ride from Kota Kinabalu, and can be reached from several other towns along the mainland coast, as well as from Bandar Seri Begawan in Brunei Darussalam.

Labuan has played an important role in the history of northern Borneo. The island occupies a strategic position at the mouth of Brunei Bay, and for a long time was part of the extensive Brunei Sultanate. In 1844, James Brooke, already White Rajah of Sarawak, was interested in obtaining Labuan for the British, as a base from which to combat piracy, increase trade and export coal from the deposits found on the island. The Sultan of Brunei eventually ceded Labuan in 1846, and although Labuan remained a British Colony, in 1890 the island came under the control of the British North Borneo Chartered Company, joining the rest of North Borneo. However in 1906, Labuan ceased to be ruled by the Chartered Company and in 1907 was placed under the government of the Straits Settlements, along with Singapore, Malacca and Penang.

After being occupied by the Japanese in the Second World War, Labuan again became part of the colony of North Borneo in 1946, but in 1963 acquired independence from Britain, became part of Sabah and joined the Federation of Malaysia. In 1984, Labuan was ceded from Sabah and was declared a Federal Territory of Malaysia.

The plaque to mark possession of Labuan Island by the British in 1846.

A Japanese memorial stone in Peace Park.

Japanese Surrender Point.

Allied War Memorial and war graves.

The Second World War had a major impact on Labuan. The Japanese seized control of the island in 1942, changing its name to Maida Island, after the Japanese Supreme Commander, Marquis Maida.

In 1945 the Japanese surrendered to the Allied Forces, commanded by Major General George F. Wootten, General Officer Commanding, 9th Australian Division. The Instrument of Surrender was signed on 10th September 1945, at Surrender Point on Labuan Island.

Rows of war graves in the Allied War Memorial mark the death of 3,992 Allied War dead. The War Memorial is a short ride away from the island's main town Victoria. At 90 sq.km., Labuan is easily visited in a day, but has some pleasant beaches for those who wish to stay longer and make use of tax-free shopping in the duty-free port.

Labuan is also an important sea port with a fine harbour and anchorage, and boasts a shipyard and an oil terminal. Natural gas occurs along with the crude oil found offshore, and is used in the production of hot iron briquettes, methanol and power.

# Introduction to Brunei Darussalam

**S**ituated between Sabah and Sarawak is the sovereign state of Brunei Darussalam. With an area of some 5,765 sq. km, Brunei is almost fifteen times the size of Singapore and five times the size of Hong Kong. Part of Sarawak divides Brunei into two separate enclaves, the larger western portion including the capital Bandar Seri Begawan and the other main towns of Kuala Belait and Tutong. The eastern section of Temburong is less populated, and accessible from the rest of Brunei only by boat.

The wide coastal plain in Temburong rises to Brunei's highest mountain, Bukit Pagon, at 1,841 metres, while most of western Brunei is hilly lowland intersected by rivers descending to the South China Sea.

Brunei's extensive mangrove and nipa palm stands along the 160 km coastline remain in relatively good condition; Proboscis Monkeys and crocodiles can still be seen here, the mangroves also providing an important breeding ground for valuable fish, prawn and crab populations.

Mangrove and nipa palms fringing one of Brunei's many coastal waterways.

Over 75% of the country is still forested, including good examples of undisturbed heath and peat swamp forests. State Forest Reserves cover about 37% of the land area. Because of the abundance of Brunei's other natural resources, oil and gas, exploitation of the forest has so far been minimal, and timber is cut for domestic use only.

Brunei's annual rainfall of around 3000 mm is similar to that in neighbouring Sabah and Sarawak, with the monsoon months of November to February usually the wettest.

Brunei is divided into four Districts: Brunei-Muara, Temburong, Tutong and Belait, each administered by a District Officer. Islam is the official religion, but other faiths including Christianity and Buddhism are also practised. As in Sabah and Sarawak, Malay is the official language, with English widely understood, and native dialects spoken in the interior.

Brunei Darussalam is a Malay Muslim Monarchy. His Majesty the Sultan and Yang Di-Pertua is the Head of State and Prime Minister, with the Royal Palace, the Istana Nurul Iman, as the seat of Government.

**T**he seemingly endless expanse of rainforest in Brunei's interior contrasts sharply with the well developed coastal belt with its prosperous towns and busy highways. Infact the main population centres are all in the coastal areas, including the capital Bandar Seri Begawan with its population of some 80,000. Brunei's total population is over 260,000, almost half of which is under 20 years of age.

Over two-thirds of Brunei's inhabitants are Malay, with the largest minority group being the Chinese at around 18%. Indigenous groups such as the Ibans, Muruts and Dusuns comprise about 5% of the population, with Europeans, Indians and other nationalities making up the remainder. There is also a large contingent of immigrant labourers, coming mainly from Thailand, Malaysia and the Philippines

Students in Kampung Ayer.

Brunei Malays share many characteristics with the Malays of Malaysia and Indonesia, having a common religion - Islam, and a preference for living in coastal areas. Their Malay dialect and customs are different enough however for them to be considered locally as a distinct ethnic gorup. Traditionally fishermen, craftsmen and traders, many of Brunei's Malays live in Kampung Ayer on the Brunei River.

Another Islamic group sharing a similar dialect to the Brunei Malays, are the Kedayans. They are traditionally rice farmers of the low hills and coastal plains.

Brunei's second largest ethnic group, the Chinese, arrived mainly within the last 100 years, from China, Hong Kong, Sarawak and Sabah. They dominate the urban commercial and business sectors and a small number have become successful vegetable farmers.

The Bisayas, including the indigenous Dusuns and Tutongs, are found in the interior areas of Tutong and Belait Districts. Previously pagan, many have converted to Christianity or Islam. Those that live in the hills are rice growers, whilst the sub-coastal Bisayas process sago.

There are a handful of Penans remaining in Brunei, most of whom have now adopted a settled way of life, cultivating both wet and hill rice, and sago palm. The Penans still hunt for meat and produce finely crafted blowpipes and baskets.

The 'Billionth Barrel' Monument at Seria

Only a few hundred Muruts still inhabit the interior, living mainly in longhouses along the upper reaches of the Temburong River. They also farm rice and are expert hunters and river fishermen.

Brunei's Iban population began filtering into the country from Sarawak in the early 1900's. Many came to work in the burgeoning oil industry, and then remained in Brunei to farm, living in longhouses chiefly on the Temburong and Belait Rivers. Like the Muruts and Bisayas, the Ibans are hill rice growers. Many have converted to Islam or Christianity, but traditional rituals, particularly those pertaining to the all important rice harvest, are still observed.

**B**runei owes its position as one of the most wealthy countries in the world, to the discovery in 1929 of onshore oil deposits, near the town of Seria at the western end of the country. Rapid and sustained expansion of the oil industry took place in the post-war years, and offshore production began in 1964. Current output is maintained at some 150,000 barrels of crude oil a day; reserves are estimated to last into the next century, and new oil fields are still being explored. A monument to mark production of the billionth barrel of crude oil was erected in Seria in 1991.

Brunei is also the world's fourth biggest producer of liquified natural gas, production of which started in 1955. The gas industry became of major importance when a large liquified natural gas plant was set up at Lumut on the west coast in 1973.

Oil production is carried out by the Brunei Shell Petroleum Company which is 50% owned by the government. Most of Brunei's crude oil is exported to other ASEAN countries, Japan and Korea, with almost all of the liquified gas going to Japan.

Oil and gas continue to provide the vast majority of Brunei's total export earnings, however Brunei is seeking to diversify its economic base away from a dependence on oil and gas in the future.

One potential resource not yet exploited is Brunei's white silica sand, an estimated 20 million tonnes of which lie on Brunei's long beaches. The brilliant white sand is thought to be ideal for glass making, and has potential use in the computer industry for Silicon chip production.

Due to the vast wealth accrued from oil and gas revenues, Bruneians enjoy one of the highest standards of living in the world, with an annual per capita income exceeding US$16,000. Residents do not pay personal income tax and enjoy free primary and secondary education and medical care.

**B**runei's relatively small size is more than made up for by its present wealth and long and fascinating history. Its official name of 'Brunei Darussalam' literally means 'Brunei Abode of Peace', and comes from an Arabic translation of the title 'Country of Lasting Tranquility', given to Brunei by the Chinese in the 1400's.

Records show that contact between Brunei and China already existed as early as the 7th or 8th century AD, when Brunei was known to the Chinese as 'Po-li' or 'Pu-ni'. It is thought that a settlement - probably a water village - already existed somewhere on the Brunei River at this time.

Early Bruneians were able seafarers, using boats with bamboo masts and sails made from tree bark. The natural port of Brunei Bay was to prove one of the most important in South East Asia, and central to the development of the Brunei empire. The regime of the north east and south west monsoons was also critical to Brunei's trading activities in the area. In the 1500's a boat from Brunei could arrive in Malacca within a month, sailing on the north east winds, and return later, loaded with traded items, during the south west monsoon season.

One of the most important and valuable exports at that time was camphor - the crystallised sap of the 'kapur' tree. North Borneo long had the reputation of producing the best camphor in the world, and to the Chinese and Indians who believed in its curative properties, Brunei's camphor was worth more than its weight in gold.

Other jungle produce traded included bees' wax, damar (sticky sap burnt in lamps), exotic birds' feathers, rhino horn and hornbill casques, and possibly not till much later, cave swiftlets' nests for the famous delicacy birds' nest soup. These items were collected by the indigenous tribes people living in the forested interior. Gold, diamonds and pepper were also exported. In return, Brunei imported commodities like brass, iron, beads, Chinese ceramics and Indian cloth.

During the 9th and 10th centuries, Brunei came under the sphere of the Buddhist Sumatran-based Srivijaya empire, and later, the Majapahit Hindu empire, centered in Java.

As the Majapahit empire declined, and with the advent of Muslim traders from the Middle East and India, Islam increased its hold in the area. Muslims came to power in Sumatra, Java, the Malay peninsula and Sulu in the southern Philippines, finally spreading their influence to coastal Borneo. The first ruler of Brunei to convert to Islam was Awang Alak Betatar, who married a Johore princess in 1368, and assumed the title Sultan Muhammad.

This began what is generally regarded as the golden age of the Brunei empire, reaching its zenith in the 16th century when Brunei extended its control to large parts of coastal Borneo and the present day Philippines. The most famous ruler of this time was Sultan Bolkiah, the 5th Sultan, who ruled in the early 1500's. Records show a highly organised system of government was in place, and that the population was already specialised in various trades and crafts such as boat building, weaving and brass-ware making.

The restored mausoleum of Sultan Bolkiah V, now a major tourist attraction.

Brunei Museum, on the site of the ancient capital Kota Batu

In 1521, the fleet of the Spanish explorer Magellan limped into Brunei harbour, minus Magellan who had been killed in the Philippines. On board was chronicler Antonio Pigafetta, who visited the resident Sultan and described a court of great opulence. The Sultan's palace was then situated at Kota Batu (Stone Fort), about 6.5 km downriver from the present capital Bandar Seri Begawan.

The leadership of the Islamic faith in South East Asia had passed to Brunei's Sultans in 1511, after the fall of Malacca to the Portuguese. In the late 1500's, Spanish influence in the area also increased, with Spain conquering the Philippines and unsuccessfully attacking Brunei in 1578.

A century later, Brunei's empire crumbled further, with a war of succession in the Sultanate and the increasing power of the Dutch in south and west Borneo. Trade decreased and with it wealth and military influence. Piracy became rife and the Sultanate continued to be wracked by internal conflict for the next 150 years.

In 1841, Brunei ceded its distant district of Sarawak to the Englishman James Brooke, in return for his help in stemming the rebellion there. And in 1846 the island of Labuan, another part of Brunei territory, was ceded to the British Crown. Brooke became the first Consul-General for Borneo and Governor of Labuan, as well as Rajah of Sarawak. Slowly the White Rajahs gained control over other parts of Brunei, and in 1890 the cession of Limbang to Sarawak saw the dividing of Brunei into two separate parts. In 1888 Brunei had become a British protectorate, along with Sarawak and North Borneo, giving Britain effective control over the entire northern area of Borneo.

In 1906, Brunei accepted a British Resident who advised the Sultan on all matters except the Islamic faith and Malay custom; the succession of the Brunei ruling dynasty was also assured. This continued until 1959,

apart from three years during the Second World War, when Brunei was occupied by the Japanese, and the capital subsequently bombed by the Allied Forces.

Brunei resumed full internal sovereignty in 1959, with Britain remaining responsible only for defense and foreign affairs, and on 1st January, 1984, full independence from Britain was gained, after nearly 100 years as a protectorate.

Brunei decided against joining the Federation of Malaysia, and proudly maintains its tradition of never having been a colony and of possessing over 500 years of Brunei Royal Family rule.

Arriving in Brunei by boat, one cannot fail to notice the hundreds of houses built on stilts over the water, clustered around a large bend in the Brunei River. This the the famous KAMPUNG AYER, which literally means 'water village', home to more than 30,000 people who live their daily lives over and around the tidal river.

Described variously as 'the Venice of the East', 'picturesque and practical', and 'imposing and magnificent', Kampung Ayer has played a central role in Brunei's long history.   Currently the largest water village in the world, the number of inhabitants of Kampung Ayer has fluctuated greatly over the centuries, mirroring the varied fortunes of Brunei itself.

Kampung Ayer was already established as the major population centre of Brunei well before the 16th century, and may have contained 20,000 - 30,000 people even then.   When Pigafetta visited Brunei in 1521, he observed that *'The City is entirely built in salt water, except the houses of the king and certain chiefs.... The houses are all constructed of wood and built up from the ground on tall pillars.  When the tide is high, women go in boats through the settlement selling articles necessary to maintain life'*.

School children going to Friday prayer.

Superficially, little has changed today.  The houses are still largely made of wood, though many now have corrugated metal roofs, and some of the labyrinth of almost 30 km of wooden walkways joining the houses have been replaced by concrete.

In the past Kampung Ayer was in fact composed of several villages, each village traditionally inhabited by people of the same occupation, such as brassware makers, fishermen, boat builders or silversmiths, and each village having its own headman.  Nowadays the divisions between the villages have become less distinct, as economic specialisation has been lost and inhabitants have inter-married with those of other villages.

Residents of Kampung Ayer commute daily to the mainland by water taxi.

Kampung Ayer remains the main residential community of Brunei, with all modern facilities including electricity and piped water supplies and its own clinics and schools.

Many inhabitants are now office workers and travel across to the town of Bandar Seri Begawan on one of the numerous 'water taxis', which zoom with amazing speed and dexterity through the maze of waterways and across the Brunei River, causing the water to be eternally choppy.

Many of Kampung Ayer's residents also have their own cars parked in parking lots along the water front; indeed Brunei has one of the highest car ownership rates in the world. However, water taxis, fishing boats and the larger passenger boats with covered cabins are still a major feature of Brunei's coastal regions.

Water taxi station on the tidal Brunei River.

Brunei has a strong history of handicraft production, including brocade weaving, silversmithing and brassware making. In recent years, as more people turned to office jobs, these skills were in danger of dying out. However, in the mid 1970's, the Brunei Arts and Handicraft Training Centre was established to teach the younger generation traditional crafts. The Centre is run by the Brunei Museum and today fine artefacts are produced, such as brass gongs and cannons, ornamental 'kris' (wavy-bladed daggers) and hand-tooled silver jewellery. The famous hand-woven brocade 'kain songket' or 'jong sarat', containing gold or silver thread and traditionally woven by women, is still widely sought after and often worn on ceremonial occasions, some pieces being extremely valuable family heirlooms.

The present capital of Brunei is situated 5 km from the mouth of the Brunei River, opposite Kampung Ayer. It was renamed BANDAR SERI BEGAWAN (Retired Nobleman's Town), in honour of the Seri Begawan Sultan, Sir Omar Ali Saifuddien, the present Sultan's father. Bandar Seri Begawan boasts a number of interesting buildings such as Parliament House and the Royal Ceremonial Hall. Also well worth a visit is the Brunei Museum, situated about 6 km from the town centre, on the site of the ancient capital of Brunei, Kota Batu.

Morning rush-hour on Kianggeh River.

Many products such as fresh fish and vegetables are still sold by vendors on the waterways.

The imposing Omar Ali Saifuddien Mosque dominating the skyline.

The Royal Barge and Omar Ali Saifuddien Mosque.

One of the most imposing buildings in Bandar Seri Begawan is the beautiful Omar Ali Saifuddien Mosque, named after the last Sultan and completed in 1958, during his reign. The Mosque overlooks Kampung Ayer and has a distinctive gold dome rising to a height of 52 metres and covered with more than 3 million pieces of Venetian mosiac. A 54-metre high minaret stands next to the dome, and adjoining the mosque is a lagoon with a concrete reconstruction of a 16th century Royal Barge. The outside walls of the mosque are coated with granite chips imported from Shanghai, while inside the walls and floor are of Italian marble.

The main market in Bandar Seri Begawan is located along the banks of the Kianggeh River, where locally prepared food dishes, fruit and vegetables, flowers and handicrafts are sold. The night market here is particularly popular. Bandar Seri Begawan is small enough to explore on foot, and with its extremely low crime rate, is one of the safest capital cities in the world.

Situated just outside Bandar Seri Begawan on a hilltop overlooking the Brunei River, is the Sultan's palace, the Istana Nurul Iman. One third of a mile long and with some 1,788 rooms, it is thought to be the world's largest residential palace currently in occupation. Amongst its superlatives the palace boasts 12 of the world's biggest chandeliers, each weighting over 2,000 kg. and two enormous golden domes covered in 22-carat gold leaf. Istana Nurul Iman was constructed in 1984, in time for Brunei's Independence celebrations. It is generally closed to the public except on special occasions such as Hari Raya Puasa.

Vegetable market at Jalan Kianggeh.

The Arts and Crafts Centre overlooking Brunei River.

The Royal Palace, Istana Nurul Iman.

The palace is home to His Majesty Sultan Haji Hassanal Bolkiah Mu'izzaddin Waddauluh, who is 29th in a royal line some believe goes back longer than any other surviving royal lineage.

His Majesty Sultan Haji Hassanal Bolkiah ascended the throne in 1967, on the voluntary abdication of his father, the late Sir Omar Ali Saifuddien, and enjoys great respect and loyalty from the people of Brunei.

Livestock market.

# Introduction to Sarawak

At approximately 124,000 sq.km, Sarawak is by far the largest state in Malaysia, constituting more than a third of the total land mass of the country. Situated on the north west side of the island of Borneo, just a few degrees above the equator, Sarawak shares its borders with Kalimantan, Brunei Darussalam and Sabah, and possesses a coastline stretching over 700 km.

It is a landscape dominated by rivers. The largest river in Sarawak - indeed in Malaysia - is the mighty Rajang, some 564 km in length. Several of Sarawak's large river systems are navigable by boat far into the interior, and all the rivers drain into the South China Sea. Due to the rugged nature of the terrain, roads are relatively few, thus rivers play a pivotal role, providing a source of transport and communication, as well as food and drinking water and bathing facilities.

Rivers are the life-blood of Sarawak; the Kenyah and Kayan people call them 'the juice of the pineapple', (pineapples being a popular fruit amongst the highland dwellers); 'silver snake' or 'rain stream' are other names also used.

Near the coast are flat plains with extensive forested peat swamps, and low hills. In the interior are rugged hills and mountain ranges, covered by rainforest. Sarawak's tallest mountain is Gunung Murud at 2,423 metres, situated in the north of the state near the border with Kalimantan.

Traders' Cave, Niah National Park.

Sarawak is noticeably humid, with the humidity often greater than 75% and higher still inside the forest. It is here that the already prodigious rainfall of Sarawak is at its highest - up to 5,000 mm a year, greater than anywhere else in Malaysia. This heavy rainfall has led to the leaching of minerals from the steep slopes, rendering the soils highly infertile and contributing to the low human population found in these areas. The heavy rain has also helped create some of the most spectacular limestone caverns in the world, including the still-being-explored Gunung Mulu cave system, and the world famous Niah Caves.

The first Europeans to visit Borneo in the early 16th century found the area of Borneo that was later to become Sarawak, part of the domain of the Sultan of Brunei, who controlled most of the coast of Borneo and the southern Philippines. This area continued under the influence of Brunei until the arrival of an Englishman, one James Brooke, in 1839.

Brooke, an adventurer out to seek his fortune (and later to become the model for Joseph Conrad's 'Lord Jim'), landed at what is now Santubong, at the mouth of the Sarawak River. He found the land to be in a state of turmoil, with Malays and Land Dayaks (Bidayuhs) rebelling against their Brunei rulers, and piracy on the seas rife.

Brooke helped the Brunei rulers to restore order and quash the rebellion. For this the Sultan of Brunei rewarded him with the title Rajah of Sarawak in 1841. The name 'Sarawak' was taken from the Sarawak River, upon which Brooke founded his capital, Kuching, about 20 miles upstream from the coast. A form of direct government for the people was introduced, which was generally considered as benevolent. Headhunting and piracy were effectively subdued.

James Brooke was succeeded by his nephew Charles Brooke in 1868. During Charles' reign Sarawak was accorded British protection, and in 1917 Charles Brooke's eldest son Charles Vyner Brooke took over position as the Rajah of Sarawak.

Japanese forces occupied Sarawak during the Second World War, interning European inhabitants in Prisoner of War camps near Kuching. At the end of the war, Sarawak was reoccupied by Australian forces, Kuching fortuitously being relatively unscathed by bombing attacks.

In 1946, after a dynasty lasting more than 100 years, the last Rajah, Charles Vyner Brooke, ceded Sarawak to the Crown, and Sarawak became a British Crown Colony, ruled by a Governor. On 16th September 1963, Sarawak achieved independence from Britain and joined the the Federation of Malaysia.

Charles Brooke Memorial in Kuching.

Undoubtedly one of the main attractions of Sarawak is its people, a mixture of over 20 ethnic groups each with their own customs, dialects and history, and famed for their warmth and hospitality.

Of a population of over 1.7 million, the Ibans constitute the dominant group at 29.5% followed by the Chinese at 28.9%, Malays 20.9%, Bidayuh 8.4%, Melanaus 5.8% and other groups including the Orang Ulu (people of the interior), 6.5%

The Malays and Melanaus are largely coastal people, while the Ibans, Bidayuhs, Kenyahs, Kayans and Bisayas occupy mostly lowland areas. The uplands are inhabited by the Kelabit, Penan and Lun Bawang.

The Chinese are the most recent immigrants to Sarawak, arriving in considerable numbers over the last 100 years, although trade connections have existed with China for 1000 years or more. They are now found throughout Sarawak as traders or merchants, but concentrated in the larger towns playing an important role in the business communities.

Around the 14th and 15th centuries, Islam found its way to Peninsular Malaysia and then Borneo, probably brought mainly by Arab traders from the Middle East. Muslim Malays traditionally settled along coastal areas, finding a living as fishermen and farmers. Now they also constitute a major part of the work force in Sarawak's Civil Service.

The Melanaus inhabit mostly coastal villages, and are mixed pagans, Muslims and Christians. Long ago their traditional longhouses were discarded in favour of individual Malay-style dwellings.

Today Sarawak has a democratic system of government and is ruled by two Constitutions - the State Constitution and the Federal Constitution. The Head of State is the Governor or Yang Di-Pertua Negeri, appointed by the King or Yang Di-Pertuan Agong of Malaysia. Every five years general elections are held, and a new Chief Minister appointed. Cabinet Ministers are then appointed by the Chief Minister.

Sarawak is divided into seven Divisions, each headed by a Resident. These Divisions are further divided into Districts, each administered by a District Officer based in the principal town in each District.

Evidence of colonial times can still be seen in Sarawak, both in the old buildings such as the Court House and Post Office in Kuching, and in the series of strategically placed forts dotted about the state, with ladies names such as Emma, Lily, Sylvia and Alice.

While the cat is the mascot of Kuching ('kucing' is Malay for cat), the Rhinoceros Hornbill (Buceros rhinoceros) forms the basis of the state emblem of Sarawak. Indeed Sarawak is often called 'The Land of the Hornbill'. Known in Sarawak as 'Kenyalang', the hornbill has for hundreds of years played a major part in Iban religious ceremonies, and hornbill feathers and motifs adorn many traditional costumes and handicrafts.

The cat is the 'mascot' of Kuching.

Sarawak Musuem, Kuching.

Sarawak's largest ethnic group and perhaps its most famous are the Ibans, or Sea Dayaks, so-called because the first Ibans encountered by Europeans were those who had become pirates in the coastal waters. Thought to have originated in Sumatra or Kalimantan, the Iban language is closer to Malay than that of any other indigenous group in Sarawak or Sabah. A particularly mobile and aggressive people, especially during the 18th and 19th centuries, the bravery of their warriors and their propensity for headhunting, where the taking of heads was among other things an important part of the dowry necessary for a man to obtain a bride, gave the Ibans a certain notoriety.

Today they are mainly farmers and agriculturalists, living in longhouses built next to rivers or streams. Many are still skilled hunters, making use of hunting dogs to track down wild pigs and deer in the forest. The older generation bear distinctive tattoos on their legs, chests, and arms.

With the advent of the Christian missionaries in Sarawak at the end of the Second World War, the majority of Ibans adopted Christianity as their main religion, although several pagan beliefs and traditions are still maintained.

The Bidayuhs or Land Dayaks are found inland from the coast in the southern hills and plains of Sarawak, and are thought to have originally come from Kalimantan. A large number are still pagans and live in longhouses, practising hill rice farming and the extensive use of bamboo. Several of the Bidayuh longhouses are easily accessible from Kuching.

Further inland along the middle and upper reaches of the main rivers are the Kenyah and Kayans, the largest of the Orang Ulu groups. Often living in related areas and sharing many similar characteristics, both groups believe their ancestors came from Kalimantan, however linguistically they are distinct. In the past the Kayans were also feared headhunters, and one of the major foes of the Ibans. Kayans and Kenyahs took up Christianity in the 1930's but still hold many ancient customs, such as belief in the powers of witch doctors and omens and taboos. Both groups are renowned as the best longhouse makers in Sarawak, the structures lasting for many years and often adorned with intricate hand-painted designs, and both groups have a socially stratified culture, unlike most of Borneo's peoples, with clearly defined 'nobles' and 'commoners'. Singing and dancing are very important in the social life of the Kenyah and Kayans, and smoking of the wild tobacco 'djako' is another common pastime.

Another Orang Ulu group is the Kelabits, inhabiting the remote and inaccessible highlands near the headwaters of the Baram river in northern Sarawak, and living in longhouses often built on low hills surrounded by grassland. In the past, Kelabits were partial to mammoth rice wine drinking sessions that could last several days; since taking up Christianity, however, these revelries have noticeably diminished. The Kelabit people have successfully mastered the art of wet rice farming in the fertile plains between the hills, using a complicated dykes and irrigation system, one of the most sophisticated in Borneo, and also raise water buffalo and cattle for cash income.

The Lun Bawang people formerly called Muruts, ('Murut' being derived from a word meaning 'hill'), are also wet rice farmers. Along with the Kelabits, with whom they hold similar traditional beliefs, their population was drastically reduced by the warring Kayans, and also by the defeated Japanese troops who retreated into the highlands at the end of the Second World War. Now the Lun Bawang are concentrated in the north of the state, near the borders with Sabah and Kalimantan.

The Penans are thought to number less than 10,000 in total, including those which are now fully settled or semi-nomadic.  It is thought that only a few hundred of the truly nomadic forest dwelling Penans remain, mostly in remote areas in the north of Sarawak, in the Baram, Belaga and Limbang districts.   These gentle, shy people have a knowledge of the forest which is unsurpassed, practising a way of life which is truly sustainable and in harmony with the environment.

Also sometimes classed as Orang Ulu, but inhabiting coastal areas along the lower Limbang River near Brunei Bay, are the Bisayas, also found in southern Sabah. Living not in longhouses but single family dwellings built close together, the Bisayas grow wet rice and raise water buffalo, and many also extract sago from the swamp forests along the coast.

*Rafflesia tuanmudae,* found in Sarawak.

Sarawak's major export is petroleum produced from oil fields off shore in the South China Sea, the first oil well having been drilled as long ago as 1910 in the town of Miri in northern Sarawak.  Today the national petroleum company, Petronas, together with Shell, are responsible for oil exploration, production and refining.  In 1978 a gas liquefaction plant was built at Bintulu, and liquefied natural gas now forms the second main contributor to the state economy.

Timber products are the third largest revenue earner, followed by the export of pepper.  Sarawak has long been one of the world's major producers of both black and white pepper, which is grown on the more fertile slopes and hillsides, and can tolerate Sarawak's high rainfall.   Other agricultural crops include rubber, coconut, oil palm, cocoa, coffee and tea. Sarawak also has the largest reserves of coal and bauxite in Malaysia.

Forests, including logged, primary and regrowing secondary forest, still cover about 70% of the state. Sarawak has one of the most extensive systems of parks and sanctuaries in Malaysia, although most, apart from the Lanjak Entimau Wildlife Sanctuary (1,687 sq. km) are of only modest size.  Bako, Niah, Gunung Mulu, Lambir Hills and the lesser known Gunung Gading and Similajau National Parks are fine representatives of virtually all Sarawak's habitat types.

From the historical town of Kuching, with its delightful blending of east and west and assimilation of traditional and modern, to the remotest longhouses way out in Sarawak's interior, from the rare 'padang' vegetation of Bako National Park to the soaring limestone pinnacles of Mt. Api, Sarawak is indeed full of treasures.

Kenyah ceremonial shield and wall painting.

West entrance of Great Cave.

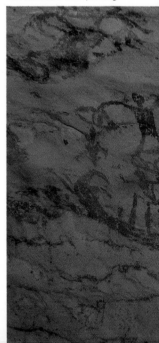

Red haematite rock painting.

**N**IAH NATIONAL PARK was gazetted in 1975, although the caves were declared a National Historic Monument as long ago as 1958. The Park is located 107 km south of Miri, off the Miri-Bintulu highway. Covering an area of 31 sq. km of lowland rainforest and limestone, the centre of attraction is the cave system comprising Great Cave, Traders' Cave and Painted Cave. At Park headquarters at Pangkalan Lobang, there is an Information Centre with exhibits on the history, archaeology, geology, flora and fauna of the Park. The caves are reached by a 4 km plankwalk through the forest and visitors arrive first at Traders' Cave, where the roofless houses of the guano and birds' nests collectors are situated.

Beyond Traders' Cave is the entrance to Great Cave. At one corner of this cave is the archaelogical site from where a 40,000 year old human skull was excavated in 1958. Inside the cave visitors can see long vertical bamboo poles stretching up to the ceiling. During the harvesting season, birds' nests collectors climb up these flimsy-looking poles to collect the nests of swiftlets that inhabit the caves.

A plankwalk and staircase lead to Gua Kira and to Painted Cave beyond. It is here that cave paintings believed to be at least 1,000 years old were discovered. These are thought to be the only red haematite rock paintings in Borneo, and depict scenes of the dead on a boat journey to the next world.

The Great Cave, Traders' Cave and Painted Cave can all be seen on a day's trip from Miri. But in order to witness the thousands of bats leaving the caves at dusk each day, it is best to stay overnight in chalets at the Park Headquarters. This will also give visitors the opportunity to explore two other trails: Jalan Madu, and Jalan Bukit Kasut which leads to the summit of Mt Subis (394 metres). It is also possible to visit Rumah Chang, a modern Iban longhouse, 15 minutes walk from the Information Centre.

Located 24 km south of Miri is LAMBIR HILLS NATIONAL PARK, an area of some 70 sq. km of forest and rugged sandstone hills.

Within these mixed dipterocarp and 'kerangas' or tropical heath forests are a number of beautiful waterfalls linked by a series of jungle trails, up to 4 hours walking distance from the Park Headquarters.

To explore the jungle trails, visitors are encouraged to stay overnight at the chalets and resthouses in the Park. A 40-metre high tree-tower on Pantu trail (1 hour) is worth a visit.

Latak waterfall, Lambir Hills National Park.

The gateway to GUNUNG (MT.) MULU NATIONAL PARK is the oil-rich town of Miri. Visitors can fly into Miri from Kuching, Bintulu, Kuala Lumpur, Labuan and Kota Kinabalu, or travel overland from Brunei Darussalam. From Miri, it is now possible to fly to Mulu in 35 minutes in a 19 seater Twin-Otter operated by Malaysia Airlines.

Fort Hose, Marudi.

A Twin-Otter operates several daily flights from Miri to Gunung Mulu National Park.

Alternatively, visitors can travel by the traditional route up the meandering Baram River by boat. The trip begins with a half-hour road journey to Kuala Baram, then a two-hour express boat journey to Marudi, a bustling little town boasting one of the oldest remaining forts built by the White Rajah to subdue piracy and head hunting in the northern part of Sarawak. The fort, named after Charles Hose and built in 1901, is now occupied by Marudi District Council. From Marudi, it is another three-hour express boat journey to Long Terawan, followed by a 45-minute ride on a longboat to Gunung Mulu National Park. The whole journey from Miri to Mulu takes the best part of a day with stops at Kuala Baram, Marudi and Long Terawan for refreshments and lunch.

For a visitor coming to Sarawak for the first time and wishing to experience a ride on one of the jumbo-shaped express boats, it is recommended to go one way to Mulu by boat, then return by air.

On approaching Gunung Mulu National Park, the longboat will pass some limestone cliffs along the Melinau River. In one of these cliffs at Batu Bungan, legend has it that a giant captured a Penan princess from the nearby jungle and held her captive in one of the caves.

Express boats at Marudi.

A typical express boat operating on Baram River.

Not far away is a modern Penan longhouse, part of a government scheme aimed at resettling the nomadic forest-dwelling Penans. Visitors can buy handicrafts including rattan baskets, mats, bangles and beaded necklaces.

Outside the Park boundary on the other side of the Melinau River are located several private lodging houses and Mulu Airport. From the lodging houses, it takes 15 minutes by speed boat to Park Headquarters which consist of an Information Centre, chalet accommodation and helipad.

Batu Bungan.

Gunung Mulu National Park Headquarters.

Gunung Mulu National Park was gazetted in 1974, but it was only in 1985 that it was opened to visitors. Its immensity and wonder was not fully appreciated until after the 15-month joint expedition of the Sarawak Government and Royal Geographical Society in 1977/78. Two further expeditions in 1980 and 1984 led to more exciting discoveries, but much more of the Park remains to be explored.

Nevertheless, the statistics of the caves discovered so far are nothing but a list of superlatives. Deer Cave, at 120 metres high and 160 metres wide, is one of the world's biggest cave passages. Sarawak Chamber is 415 metres wide by 600 metres long, with a total area of some 162,700 square metres, or 20 times the size of a football field, and a volume of 12 million cubic metres. This makes it the biggest known cave chamber in the world. Clearwater Cave is the longest cave system in South East Asia and seventh longest in the world, with over 100 km of passages mapped to date and new discoveries being made each year.

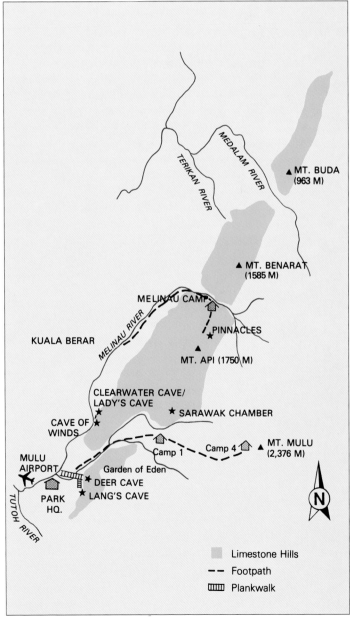

Map of Gunung Mulu National Park.

Plankwalk leading to Deer and Lang's Caves.

Lying at the end of a 3 km plankwalk, 45 minutes walk from Park Headquarters, is the southern entrance to DEER CAVE, long known to local inhabitants as a good place to hunt deer which came to the cave for salt. Looking out of the southern entrance, a profile not unlike that of Abraham Lincoln can be easily discerned in the rockface.

A 1 km concrete footpath, together with a wooden staircase on steep sections, winds through the cave passage abruptly ending at a river near the northern entrance. One must cross this river in order to go to the 'Garden of Eden', an enclosed valley of unspoilt rainforest. In several places, water seeping through from the hill above cascades from the roof of the cave, sometimes issuing from the ends of inverted funnel-shaped stalactites. Two of these are named 'Adam's Shower' and 'Eve's Shower'.

Except for the river flowing through the cave and the water cascading from the roof, the cave seems lifeless. However, close scrutiny of the bat and swiftlet droppings or guano reveals many tiny creatures, including cockroaches, earwigs, White - noodle Millipedes, moth caterpillars, beetles, crickets and mites. In the darkness where eyes are of little use, insects, centipedes, spiders, scorpions and crabs feel their way around by developing long legs or antennae.

High up in the roof of the cave passage live an estimated 750,000 bats. At dusk, a fantastic hour-long exodus unfolds as wave after wave of these Wrinkle-lipped Bats fly out to spend the night hunting for insects. Occasionally, some fall prey to eagles waiting by the cave entrance. As the bats fly out, so the swiftlets fly in, returning to the cave to roost for the night. Many visitors to the Park consider this spectacle to be the highlight of their trip.

A hiker dwarfed by a strangling fig tree along the 3 km plankwalk to Deer Cave.

Bats streaming out of Deer Cave into the evening sky.

Cave exit leading to the secret 'Garden of Eden'.

The southern entrance of Deer Cave with 120 metre high cascades.

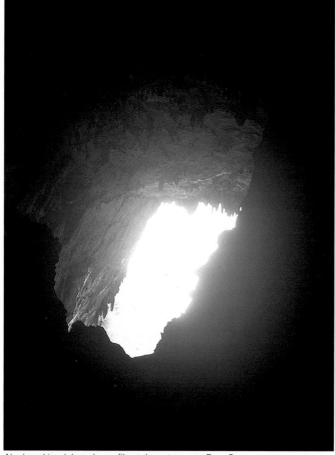

Abraham Lincoln's rocky profile at the entrance to Deer Cave.

'Eve's Shower', Deer Cave.

Stalactites inside Wind Cave.

Delicate limestone formations in Lang's Cave.

Huntsman spider, *Heteropoda sp.* Large individuals can reach 15 cm across.

King's Room inside Wind Cave.

The superb limestone formations of Lang's Cave.

**J**ust a short walk from Deer Cave is LANG'S CAVE, named after the local guide who first showed it to cavers in 1978. Unlike Deer Cave which impresses by its sheer size, Lang's Cave expresses its beauty through the masses of limestone features including stalactites, stalagmites, helictites and delicate limestone curtains.

In areas where the cave roof is low, fibreglass roofs have been constructed over the walkways to protect both visitors and stalactites alike.

**W**IND CAVE is aptly named because of the constant draft issuing from inside the cave. A short wooden walkway from the Melinau River leads to the entrance of this cave. In the upper part is the King's Room, so named due to its magnificent stalactites and stalagmites, and where the cool breeze is even more refreshing.

As in most of the show caves, special concrete or wooden walkways have been installed to facilitate walking over the sometimes slippery rock surfaces, and to prevent damage to the fragile rock formations.

Visitors arriving at a jetty on Clearwater River.

Single leafed plants *(Monophyllaea glanca)* growing at the Clea

A little upstream from Wind Cave, along a tributary of the Melinau River half an hour by longboat from Park headquarters, is CLEAR-WATER CAVE. Two hundred steps lead up to the cave entrance from the river bank, however only a tiny portion of the cave passage near the entrance is open to visitors. Through the cave flows Clearwater River, which cuts deep into the floor forming a steep-sided canyon-like channel, and notches in the cave walls. The river then emerges outside the cave where it is possible to swim and relax in the crystal-clear green coloured water.

Lady's Cave

A djoining Clearwater Cave, to the right of the entrance, is LADY'S CAVE, an example of a dry cave passage. As the cave becomes dry, stalactites and stalagmites begin to develop, along with banks of mud and gravel.

All four show caves have had lighting strategically installed to highlight spectacular rock formations and illuminate dim passages; however it is still recommended to bring along a torch for personal use.

For those who enjoy jungle trekking, it is possible to climb up MT. MULU (2,376 metres), a sandstone mountain from which the Park derives its name.

A return trip to the summit of Mt. Mulu from Park Headquarters takes 4 days. The first day's trail involves a 3-hour walk of 8 km through flat terrain to Camp 1 for an overnight stay. On Day 2, it is uphill all the way to Camp 4 at 1,800 metres. Here the vegetation is noticeably shorter and lumps of moss and lichens are common, and rhododendrons and pitcher plants especially *Nepenthes lowii* abound. From Camp 4, it is only 1 ½ hours to the summit on Day 3, before making the return journey to Camp 1 for the night. Spending a night here on Day 3 allows the climber more daylight hours on the summit. On Day 4 it is back through the lowland primary forest to Park Headquarters.

*Balanophora reflexa*, a parasitic flower common in montane forest.

trance.

*Nepenthes muluensis*, endemic to Gunung Mulu.

Mt. Api as viewed from Mt. Mulu.

Jungle trekking to Melinau Camp.

**M**T. API (1,750 metres) is the highest limestone mountain in South East Asia. Millions of years of heavy rainfall have eroded the limestone, resulting in the formation of 45 metre tall razor-shaped pinnacles about two thirds of the way up the mountain.

To see the pinnacles, it is necessary to spend two nights at Melinau Camp at the base of Mt. Api by the Melinau River. The trip includes a one hour boat journey from Park Headquarters to Kuala Berar (it takes longer in the dry season), followed by 2-3 hours (8km) trekking through lowland rainforest to Melinau Camp. The trek up and down to the pinnacles at 1,200 metres can be done in a day from here. The first 900 metres of the trek involves a steep uphill walk, while the final 300 metres consist of scrambling up sharp limestone rocks with the aid of ropes and aluminium ladders.

The inflorescence of *Amorphophallus borneensis*, which can grow up to 2m high.

Scaling the aluminium ladder at the summit of Mt. Api.

**G**unung Mulu Naitonal Park is not just about enormous caves with spectacular limestone formations. Its unique and rich flora and fauna must not be overlooked.

The exceptionally high rainfall of between 6000 - 7000 mm per year, plus the attendant high humidity, make Mulu a botanist's paradise. Over 1500 species of flowering plants have been identified, including 170 species of orchid and 10 species of pitcher plants.

The Park also contains a diverse bird population, with all eight species of hornbill represented. Butterflies (281 species) and frogs (74 species) also abound.

Mountain treeshrew on Mt. Api.

Walker Lanternfly *(Pyrops intricata)*.

The majestic limestone pinnacles of Mt. Api.

**S**IBU, the second largest town in Sarawak, is the gateway to the hinterland of the Rajang River, Sarawak's longest river. Situated at the confluence of the Rajang and Igan Rivers, Sibu's many express boats provide the main means of communication to the interior of Sarawak.

With a current population of 150,000 inhabitants, mostly of Chinese origin, settlement of the area began just over a century ago, when the White Rajah started encouraging immigration from China, resulting in the attraction of farmers from China's Foochow province. The original settlement of Sungei Merah proved too small and new immigrants moved on to Sibu, which offered a larger area for agriculture and farming. Later, other Chinese groups including Heng Hua, Hokkien, Cantonese and Teochew followed.

The interior of an express boat plying between Sibu and Kapit.

Panoramic view of the Rajang River waterfront in Sibu.

Tributaries of the Rajang River.

Detail from the roof of Tua Pek Kong pagoda temple, Sibu.

Today, Sibu is a sprawling financial and trading port. From dawn until long after the sun has set, the town is a hive of non-stop activity. At the Rajang River, rows and rows of express boats are tightly sandwiched together with more boats squeezing in to get a landing space to unload their human cargo, all assortments of fruits including durians, and live animals. From here, passengers can go upriver to Kanowit, Song, Kapit and as far as Belaga, or downriver to Igan, Bintangor, Sarikei and to Kuching. The latest express boats are aerodynamically designed, and are capable of carrying over 50 passengers at speeds of 40 knots powered by 1,000 horsepower engines. The local shipyards churning out these express boats are now generating over 50 million ringgit of revenue annually, further strengthening the local economy. As expected, the atmosphere is one of intense competition and entrepreneurship, and Sibu boasts a respectable number of millionaires. Yet on the streets, bicycles, rickshaws and motorcycles are everywhere. Sibu has the highest concentration of bicycles anywhere in Malaysia.

Behind the river pier are the local native markets, where live animals from chickens to frogs, and fresh and salted fish are sold. Nearby is a Buddhist temple with a very impressive 7-storey pagoda. The best panoramic view of the whole town and the Rajang esplanade is obtained from the top floor.

Even at night, commercial activities do not stop completely. Many shops are open until 10.00 pm and streets around the market are closed to traffic for the night markets to ply their wares, including a colourful assortment of local cakes and sweets. When in Sibu, the opportunity must not be missed to try out the famous local Foochow noodles, long-life noodles and rice noodles with cuttlefish.

Durian season at Sibu market.

Rumah Enggin longhouse near Kapit.

Young Iban girl.

**K**apit, approximately 150km upstream and about 3 hours by express boat from Sibu, is half way up the RAJANG RIVER to Belaga.

Half an hour inland from Kapit is Rumah Enggin, an Iban longhouse. Here a cluster of human skulls still hangs outside on the 'Ruai' or longhouse verandah. The Ibans in Rumah Enggin practise a mixture of Islam, Christianity and animism all under one roof.

Much of the commercial activities in this area are centred around the timber industry. Most local families have at least one member employed in the timber camps. As a result of this injection of income, longhouses are gradually becoming more modern. Some longhouses on the Baleh and Rajang Rivers are concrete double storey buildings with aluminum sliding glass windows and electricity. But inland along the smaller tributaries, life has not changed much. Mothers still do their washing and bathe children in the river each day. The whole longhouse still gathers around to welcome tourists or visitors with 'tuak' or rice wine. Hospitality is never short in coming. During the 'gawais' or festivals, the longhouse is full of people, with relatives returning to join in the festivities. Gambling, tuak drinking, dancing, merry making and cock fighting are the order of the day. On normal days, ladies will be busy making baskets and mats, weaving pua kumbu or minding their young children, while men mend their fishing nets, repair their speed boat engines and make jungle knives and baskets.

Cock fighting - a common pastime amongst the Ibans.

An Iban boy at Kanowit.

A typical scene on Katibas River.

A Kenyah lady in costume.

Kanowit jetty.

Shophouses in Kapit.

Upriver from Kapit and beyond the Pelagus Rapids live the Orang Ulus, the people of the interior. At Punan Bah can be seen some 'keliriengs', sculptured poles 10 metres tall and 2 metres in diameter. Made of belian hardwood, these were used in the old days to intern the remains of the Punan chiefs.

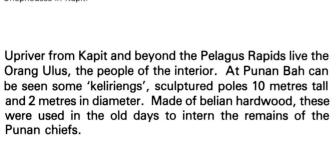

Kuching esplanade along the Sarawak River.

The Astana, built in 1870 and the offical residence of the Head of State.

**K**uching, the capital of Sarawak, the former capital of the White Rajahs and one of the first towns to be settled in northern Borneo, is truly a city of unique contrasts.

The Malay fishermen's houses along the Sarawak River provide a striking juxtaposition to the ultra modern multi-storey government offices. Not far from the imposing State Mosque across the river are located the Astana, former residence of the White Rajahs, and Fort Margherita built in 1879 by Charles Brooke and named after his wife, Ranee Margaret. Today it is a police museum.

Just as in former days, water taxis still operate across the Sarawak River, powered by two long oars with a small motor as a back-up. It is very inexpensive to travel across the river by one the numerous water taxis along the esplanade. Indeed, they are used daily by many local people to go to schools and offices from their homes across the river. Alternatively, tourists can opt for the bigger and more modern boat, the Equatorial, which runs daily tours along the Sarawak River.

Nearby is located the main tourist belt of Kuching, where big international hotels including the Holiday Inn, Riverside Majestic and Hilton are located.

Along the same road is the colourful Tua Pek Kong Chinese temple. Built in 1876, it is the oldest temple in Sarawak, and is the central place of worship for the Chinese Buddhist community in Kuching.

Many of the original old shophouses still line the streets, as unlike most of the other major towns in Borneo, Kuching was the target of only a few bombs in the Second World War and remained relatively intact, giving it an unusually historical and intriguing atmosphere.

Fort Margherita on the banks of the Sarawak River.

Not to be missed is the world-renowned Sarawak Museum, the oldest museum in Malaysia. Surrounded by lush green landscaped gardens, the museum was built in 1891 by Charles Brooke at the recommendation of the naturalist Alfred Russell Wallace. Since then the Museum collections have outgrown the building and a new block 'Dewan Tun Razak' has been constructed nearby. Within the Museum are galleries on archaeology, history, natural history and ethnography as well as model houses of the Orang Ulus. There are also unique collections of native handicrafts and priceless Chinese porcelain.

Outside in the garden are several 'keliriengs', Punan burial poles, brought down from the Belaga area. The most impressive specimen is located outside Dewan Tun Razak. Also on display are stone carvings, a 'Salong' or Kayan burial chamber and a World War II Heroes' Grave.

The Kuching Hilton as viewed from the Sarawak River, and backdrop for a traditional water taxi.

An Orang Ulu burial pole or 'kelirieng' outside

A typical shophouse along Main Bazaar.

Kuching State Mosque.

Tua Pek Kong Chinese Temple.

Sarawak pottery.

In Kuching, several Chinese pottery factories have sprung up and have successfully combined traditional oriental ceramic skills with ethnic motifs to create Sarawak's own distinctive style of pottery.

Among the ethnic groups, the Ibans are famous for their handwoven 'pua kumbu'. The Kenyah, Kayan, Kajang and Punan are renowned as the most skilled wood carvers, crafting anything from burial poles to musical instruments, as well as being well known for their skill in making longhouses and longboats. Kenyah traditional wooden face masks are particularly striking.

The Ibans, Kenyahs and Kayans also make beautiful beaded handicrafts, while the Penans produce the finest rattan baskets and sleeping mats, and the best blowpipes in Borneo.

Fairy Cave at Bau.

In the vicinity of Kuching are several places of interest which are easily accessible by road. Half an hour along the Kuching-Serian road, is Jong's Crocodile Farm, named after its owner. The farm contains over 1,000 crocodiles which are bred to supply the world demand for crocodile skins, thus relieving the pressure on wild crocodile populations, previously hunted to supply the trade. The farm breeds two species - the Estuarine Crocodile *Crocodylus porosus,* and the fresh water Malaysian Gharial — *Tomistoma schlegelii.*

Jong's Crocodile Farm.

An adolescent Orang Utan at Semonggok Orang Utan Rehabilitation Centre.

BAU, 40 km from Kuching and a former gold mining town, is home to several limestone caves one of which is known as the Fairy Cave. This cave is used by local Chinese as a place for ancestral worship. Incense altars are positioned at strategic locations, and incense sticks burnt at any limestone formation with the slightest resemblance to human or animal figures.

At SEMONGGOK, 22 km from Kuching, is Sarawak's only rehabilitation centre for Orang Utans, which, similar to Sepilok in Sabah, rescues Orang Utans from captivity or from areas where their habitat is being destroyed, and reintroduces them to the wild. Gibbons and birds such as hornbills can also be seen at the centre.

Skulls in the Head House of Bidayuh longhouse.

A pagan ceremony performed by the elders of a Bidayuh longhouse.

A 'miring' ceremony during a 'gawai' festival at Benuk.

At BENUK, 35 km from Kuching, is a Bidayuh (Land Dayak) longhouse. During ceremonies, prayers are chanted over the food by men and women dressed in red and black costumes. Next to the longhouse in a separate building, is a Head-House where human skulls are hung and brought out during festivals. The house is only open on special occasions, and is still surrounded by a great deal of superstition by the locals, especially the older generations.

Dreams and evil spirits still play an important role in the lives of the Bidayuhs, with every dream having a special significance. To dream of a fire breaking out for instance, means the village will be afflicted by an epidemic, and a dream where someone is laughing is thought to signify bad news.

**G**azetted in 1957, BAKO NATIONAL PARK is Sarawak's oldest Park. Although only 27 sq. km in size, it has an exceptionally rich and diverse flora and fauna.

Bako is only 37 km from Kuching, and can be reached by a half-hour boat ride from Kampung Bako, itself just half an hour on sealed roads from the capital.

Sunset over Santubong from Bako National Park.

'Padang' or heath vegetation on Lintang trail.

An epiphytic ant plant
(Hydnophytum formicarium).

Fiddler crab.

Sea stack, shaped by the action of the sea and wi

Weathering processes on the sandstone strata have created a coastline indented by sandy beaches with sea arches and sea stacks, and coves with steep cliff faces covered by honeycombs and pink iron patterns.

Within the Park, it is possible to see representatives of practically every type of vegetation in Borneo. Along the coastal areas are mangrove trees, thriving in shallow sea water. A plankwalk on the Lintang Trail passes through a typical mangrove forest. Further inland is the dipterocarp forest with its giant trees reaching 30 metres above the forest floor. At the highest point of the Park are stretches of shrubby 'padang' vegetation. Here, several species of pitchers including *Nepenthes ampullaria, rafflesiana, gracilis* and *albomarginata* are readily observed along the well-marked trails. Four types of the fascinating ant plants, where certain species of ants and plants live in a mutually beneficial or symbiotic relationship, can also be seen.

Silvered Leaf Monkeys *(Presbytis cristata)* amongst mangrove roots.

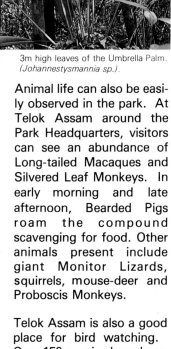
3m high leaves of the Umbrella Palm. *(Johannestysmannia sp.)*.

one.

Mangrove plankwalk on Lintang Trail.

Animal life can also be easily observed in the park. At Telok Assam around the Park Headquarters, visitors can see an abundance of Long-tailed Macaques and Silvered Leaf Monkeys. In early morning and late afternoon, Bearded Pigs roam the compound scavenging for food. Other animals present include giant Monitor Lizards, squirrels, mouse-deer and Proboscis Monkeys.

Telok Assam is also a good place for bird watching. Over 150 species have been recorded including several migrants such as plovers, wagtails, pipits, shrikes, warblers and fly catchers.

*Nepenthes rafflesiana* (aerial pitcher).

Bearded Pigs *(Sus barbatus)*.

Damai Beach Holiday Inn.

Damai Beach.

A coconut plantation at Santubong village.

**N**estled in the foothills of the legendary Mt. Santubong, 35 km north of Kuching, is the famous **DAMAI BEACH** on which is located the holiday resort of Damai Beach Holiday Inn. Visitors to the resort can relax on long sandy beaches, or participate in various water sports in the calm South China Sea.

Kenyahs playing the 'Sape' at the Orang Ulu Longhouse.

Sarawak Cultural Village and Mt. Santubong.

Within walking distance of Damai Beach is SARAWAK CULTURAL VILLAGE, a microcosm of Sarawak's rich cultural heritage, comprising typical houses of the seven major ethnic groups, built around a man-made lake which symbolises the importance of water and rivers as a source of food and means of communication to the people of Sarawak.

On show is a Bidayuh ceremonial round Head-House or 'Barok', where enemies' heads were traditionally displayed and where pagan ceremonies were performed. Weapons such as cannons, spears, shields and blowpipes can also be seen.

'Orang Ulu' is a collective term which includes the Kenyah, Kayan, Kelabit, Berawan, Kajang, Sekapan, Lun Bawang and Lun Dayeh peoples. In the Orang Ulu house, authentic Kenyah motifs decorate both the walls and pillars, on which are displayed shields, hats and ceremonial knives. Outside to welcome visitors is a Kenyah hunter with his lethal blowpipe, complete with real darts (minus the poison), cajoling visitors to test their skill.

Blow pipe demonstration outside the Orang Ulu longhouse.

An Iban lady weaving the traditional 'pua kumbu'.

The Iban longhouse is a series of family rooms with a long, communal, covered verandah or 'ruai'. Human skulls can be seen hanging over the fire place. Inside the rooms are many museum artifacts, including bronze gongs, Chinese urns and handlooms with half-finished 'pua kumbu'. Walls are made of tree bark, floors covered with rattan mats and stairs cut out of tree trunks. Visitors entering the longhouse are served with the potent rice wine, 'tuak'.

The Chinese farm house, unlike the Iban longhouse, is built on ground level, while the Malay house is constructed on stilts and boasts colourful ceremonial chambers. The windows, bannisters and roof fascia boards are all elaborately carved.

The Melanau house is built on very tall stilts, as Melanaus inhabit low lying swampy areas between the Rajang River mouth and Baram River. When attacked by pirates as often happened in earlier times, the ladders were pulled up thus providing refuge to the occupants inside.

Also shown is the simple dwelling of one of the last nomadic tribes in Sarawak, the Penan House, made of palm leaves, saplings and bark. The Penans are very skilful hunters, using their hunting dogs and blowpipes.

For any visitor to Sarawak who is in a hurry, this ' Living Museum' is an opportunity to experience a taste of the rich cultural diversity of Sarawak in half a day. But nothing can be as exciting as seeing the real thing.

Dancers in an assortment of traditional costumes.

Ibans by the river near a Batang Ai longhouse.

A 'Ngajat' or warrior dance.

For those who have the time, a visit to an Iban longhouse in the interior is well worth the effort.

One such longhouse is at Ugat, on the Engkari River deep in the interior near the Indonesian border. To reach Ugat takes the best part of a day, and involves a 232 km journey along the Kuching-Sibu highway to Sri Aman. From here it is a short drive to the BATANG AI hydroelectric dam and then a relaxing motorised boat trip across the reservoir to the Engkari River, one of the tributaries of the Batang Ai.

At the longhouse, visitors are accommodated in a nearby resthouse built by one of the tour operators from Kuching.

Iban lady with spindle.

Pounding rice to remove the husks is still a daily chore.

Iban girls in traditional dress at a Skrang River

Pepper plantation at Serian.

Drying black pepper on a longhouse verandah.

Skilful boatmen manoeuvering two long boats through a shallow stretch of the Skrang River.

**E**nroute to the Batang Ai, SKRANG and LEMANAK RIVERS, pepper plantations line the side of the Kuching – Sibu highway. Pepper is now widely grown as a cash crop in addition to padi, rubber and cocoa. The pepper vines are grown up and around 3-5 metre long belian poles on hillsides, and when collected, the pepper is laid out on longhouse verandahs to dry.

Similar to the latter part of the journey to Ugat longhouse at Batang Ai, a trip up the Lemanak or Skrang Rivers reveals crystal clear and sometimes very shallow water, running through beautiful overhanging rainforest. During the dry season, the shallow water occasionally means everyone must disembark and help to push the boat up river. Lying back in one of these 5-7 seater longboats and watching the skill of the Iban boatmen negotiating the shallow waters whilst taking in the cool breeze and the sweet sound of jungle, is an unforgettable experience.

A finished Iban necklace.

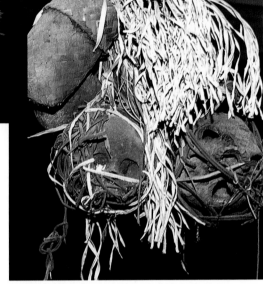

A variety of handicrafts is offered for sale in the longhouses, including bangles, parangs, woven baskets and hats and old Chinese pottery.

Some of the beads used in the Iban ceremonial necklaces may be centuries old and very valuable. In the past they were used as currency, bridal wealth or decoration and sometimes buried with the dead. The ancient beads were mostly made of glass and of Chinese origin.

Human skulls hanging from the roof of Murat longhouse, Skrang River.

Handicrafts for sale at Kesit longhouse, Lemanak River.

An Iban elder in warrior regalia.

Winnowing padi.

Boat making at Murat longhouse.

In Sarawak's longhouses, life goes on, balancing the old and the new, cherishing traditions that have existed for centuries.

As in Sabah and Brunei Darussalam, Sarawak takes pride in its rich and varied cultural heritage, ensuring that traditional skills are not lost.

The natural heritage is of equal importance, people depending on Borneo's great rainforests and the surrounding seas for food, to regulate climate, for water, for building materials, for spiritual upliftment, and much, much more.

Let us hope that a greater appreciation of the beauty and fragility of the ecology and cultures of Borneo, will engender a vision to ensure a sustainable and fulfilling future for Borneo and all its people.

Ibans dressed up for a festival.

The delicate art of wood carving on a longhouse verandah.

# Acknowledgements

The publisher and photographer of this book wishes to thank the following:-

**Kuala Lumpur:** YB Dato' Sabbaruddin Chik, Minister of Culture, Arts and Tourism, Malaysia;

**Sabah:** YB Tham Nyip Shen, Minister of Tourism and Environmental Development; Datuk Tan Kit Sher, Chairman, Sabah Tourism Promotion Corporation; Datuk Wilfred Lingham; Datuk Tengku Zainal Adlin, Deputy Director, Sabah Foundation; Datuk Lamri Ali, Director, Sabah Parks; Datuk Mohamad Gan, Semporna Ocean Tourism Centre; Irene Charuruks, General Manager, Sabah Tourism Promotion Corporation; Francis Liew, Deputy Director, Sabah Parks; Dr. Clive Marsh, Assistant General Manager (Conservation & Environmental Services), Innoprise Corporation Sdn Bhd; Patrick Andau, Director, Wildlife Department; Dr. Junaidi Payne, Co-ordinator, WWF Sabah; Tony Liew, General Manager, Sabah Air; Patricia Regis, Director, Sabah Museum; Joanna Kitingan, Director, Sabah State Archives; Jessie Chevrez, General Manager, Sandakan Renaissance Hotel; Tan Vun Heong, Manager, Hotel Hsiang Garden, Sandakan; David Sia, Proprietor, Supreme Art Foto; Jamili Nais, Ecologist, Kinabalu Park; Tony Lamb and Anthea Phillipps;

**Brunei Darussalam:** Cany and Paula Mah, Sunshine Borneo Tours; Alex Teo, Capital Hotel; Mark McWhinnie, General Manager, Sheraton Utama Hotel;

**Sarawak:** YB Datuk Amar James Wong, Minister of Environment and Tourism; Denis Hon, Permanent Secretary, Ministry of Environment and Tourism; Gavin and Dunstan Lee, Interworld Travel, Kuching; Jimmy Choo, CPH Travel Agencies, Kuching; Wolfgang Maier, General Manager, Hilton Kuching; Shamsir S.Askor, General Manager, Holiday Inn Damai Beach; Alexander Linggi, Hotel Meligai, Kapit; Johnny Wong, Sarawak Hotel Travel Department, Sibu; Stanley Malang, Borneo Overland Services, Miri;

**Labuan:** Willie Teo, Tradewings International;

and all the other friends and colleagues who have helped in one way or another in the production of this book.

Sabah Dragon Boat Festival.

# Picture Credits

**Tengku Adlin** Pg.39 *(Rafflesia tengku-adlinii)*

**Daniel D'Orville, Borneo Divers** Pg.86 (turtle cavern); Pg.87 (snorkeler); Pg.87 (sunset); Pg.87 (turtle)

**Tommy Chang** Pg.22 (boulder coral, feather star, clown fish) Pg.53 (sunrise)

**Andreas Driza, Club Montée** Pg.61-62 (rock climbing)

**Charles Francis** Pg.52 (Green Imperial Pigeon); Pg.71 (lizard); Pg.79 (Mossy-nest Swiftlet); Pg.79 (White-nest Swiftlet); Pg.79 (Lesser Woolly Horseshoe Bat); Pg.82 (Reddish Scops Owl); Pg.82 (Black-throated Babbler); Pg.114 *(Balanophera reflexa)*; Pg.114 *(Nepenthes muluensis)*; Pg.115 (Mt. Api)

**Susan K. Jacobson** Pg.63 (frogs)

**Clement Lee, Borneo Divers** Pg.86 (Spotted Sweet-lips); Pg.88 (feather star)

**Clive Marsh** Pg.84 (fungus); Pg.84 (Danum Valley Field Centre)

**Jamili Nais** Pg.63 (Indigo Flycatcher); Pg.63 (Rajah Brooke's Birdwing Butterfly)

**Poon Wai Ming** Pg.35 *(Rafflesia pricei)*; Pg.63 *(Eurema sp)*; Pg.82 (Night Heron)

**Sabah State Archives** Pg.5 (map)

**Sandakan Renaissance Hotel** Pg.70 (hotel)

**David Sia** Pg.49 (Murut dancers)

**Anwar Sullivan** Pg.33 (Rungus lady)

**Hj. Yacob Dato Paduka Hj. Sunny** Pg.31-32 (Tempasuk Plain)

**Tham Yau Kong** Pg.39 *(Nepenthes trusmadiensis)* Pg.64 *(Nepenthes rajah)*

**Ag. Mokti Ag. Tuah** Pg.83 (tree tower)

**Voon Joon Hee** Pg.104 *(Rafflesia tuanmudae)*; Pg.115 *(Amorphophallus)*

**Mohd. Zaini Wahab** Pg.66 *(Rafflesia keithii)*

**Sylvia Yorath** Pg.86 (Sipadan Island)

All other photographs by **Albert C. K. Teo**

# Further Reading

**Sabah - Land of the Sacred Mountain** by Albert C.K. Teo; text by A. G. Sullivan. (1990)

**A Guide to Sandakan, Sabah, Malaysia** by Albert C.K. Teo; text by Dr. Junaidi Payne. (1990)

**A Guide to the Parks of Sabah** by Anthea Phillipps. Sabah Parks Publication No. 9. (1988)

**Exotic Islands of Tunku Abdul Rahman Park** by Albert C.K. Teo; text by Anthea Phillipps. (1989)

**Kinabalu Park** by Susan Kay Jacobson. Sabah Parks Publication No. 7. (1986)

**Rhododendrons of Sabah** by G. Argent, A. Lamb, A. Phillipps, S. Collenette; Sabah Parks Publication No. 8. (1988)

**Rafflesia - Magnificent Flower of Sabah** by Kamarudin Mat Salleh. (1991)

**Nepenthes of Mount Kinabalu** by Shigeo Kurata; Sabah Parks Publication No. 2. (1976)

**Orang Utan - Malaysia's Mascot** by Junaidi Payne and Mahedi Andau. (1989)

**Wild Malaysia** - photographs by Gerald Cubitt, text by Junaidi Payne. (1990)

**Sabah - The Land Below the Wind** by Peter Chay. (1988)

**Sabah** - by Robert Hoebel. (1984)

**Sabah, Borneo** by Wendy Hutton; Insight Pocket Guides. (1992)

**Sipadan - Borneo's Underwater Paradise** by Michael Patrick Wong. (1991)

**Sabah's History in Pictures (1881 - 1981)** by Johan M. Padasian. (1981)

**Under Chartered Company Rule (North Borneo 1881-1946)** by K.G. Tregonning. (1958)

**Land Below the Wind** by Agnes Keith. (1948)

**Three Came Home** by Agnes Keith. (1948)

**A Guide to Brunei Darussalam** by Albert C.K. Teo; text by Nigel Coventry. (1992)

**European Sources for the History of the Sultanate of Brunei in the Sixteenth Century.** Edited by Robert Nicholl. Brunei Museum. (1975)

**Sarawak** by Hedda Morrison. (1976)

**Sarawak** by Robert Hoebel. (1989)

**Giant Caves of Borneo** by Mike Meredith and Jerry Wooldridge with Ben Lyon. (1992)

**Birds of Borneo** by Bertram E. Smythies. (1981)

**Pocket Guide to the Birds of Borneo.** Compiled by Charles M. Francis. (1984)

**A Field Guide to the Mammals of Borneo** by Junaidi Payne, Charles M. Francis and Karen Phillipps. (1985)

# Index